Studies in Writing & Rhetoric

Other Books in the Studies in Writing & Rhetoric Series

Rehearsing New Roles

Rehearsing New Roles

How College Students
Develop as Writers

Lee Ann Carroll

SOUTHERN ILLINOIS UNIVERSITY PRESS

Carbondale and Edwardsville

All rights reserved
Printed in the United States of America
  05 04 03 02   4 3 2 1
Publication partially funded by a subvention grant from The Conference on
College Composition and Communication of the National Council of Teachers of
English.

    Library of Congress Cataloging-in-Publication Data

    Carroll, Lee Ann, 1946–
      Rehearsing new roles : how college students develop as writers / Lee Ann
    Carroll.
        p. cm. — (Studies in writing & rhetoric)
      Includes bibliographical references and index.
        1. English language—Rhetoric—Study and teaching. 2. Report
    writing—Study and teaching (Higher). I. Title. II. Series.
    PE1404 .C346 2002
    808'.042'0711—dc21
    ISBN 0–8093–2449–0 (pbk. : alk. paper)   2002018755

Printed on recycled paper. ♻

The paper used in this publication meets the minimum requirements of American
National Standard for Information Sciences—Permanence of Paper for Printed
Library Materials, ANSI Z39.48–1992. ♾

To my father, John Carroll, with thanks, and in memory of my mother, Elva Vollmer Carroll

Contents

Preface

> The developmental importance of ecological transitions derives
> from the fact that they almost invariably involve a change in
> *role,* that is in the expectations for behavior associated with
> particular positions in society. Roles have a magiclike power to
> alter how a person is treated, how she acts, what she does, and
> thereby even what she thinks and feels.
> —Urie Bronfenbrenner, *The Ecology of Human Development*

"**W**e can help you to be a better writer." This writing center slogan
displayed on posters across a college campus implies a theory of
development that writers can indeed become "better" and provides
an assurance that the writing center is an environment that promotes such development. Composition specialists in all the many
roles they play operate from either tacit or explicit theories of development and owe their professional careers to the assumption that
they know something about how to help people become better writers. They are called on as experts to help dispel myths about writing and to suggest effective teaching strategies to faculty across the
curriculum. But what do we actually know about how the writing of
students develops over the course of several years of college? This
longitudinal study attempts to answer this question for a group of
20 students at a midsize independent university by following their
development as writers over four years.

While some college faculty members and administrators cling
to the myth that adequately prepared students should be able to
write fluently and correctly on any topic, at any time, in any context, this study demonstrates that even students who were generally
successful in high school are unable to fulfill this fantasy. I want to
demonstrate in this volume why a one- or two-semester, first-year
course in writing cannot meet all the needs of even our more experienced writers and show how students' complex literacy skills

develop slowly, often idiosyncratically, over the course of their college years, as they choose or are coerced to take on new roles as writers.

Our study students did not necessarily learn to write "better," but they did learn to write differently—to produce new, more complicated texts, addressing challenging topics with greater depth and complexity. They showed development as writers in terms defined by Scardamalia (1981), when she writes, "much of the story of cognitive development may be construed as taking progressively more variables into account during a single act of judgment" (p. 82; quoted in Walvoord & McCarthy, 1990, p. 13). They became better able to juggle the multiple literacy acts often required by the commonplace writing assignments of college courses.

The work of our study students demonstrates that the "basic skills" necessary to negotiate complex literacy tasks in college go far beyond the ability to produce grammatically correct, conventional, thesis-driven schoolroom essays. I argue that understanding the literacy demands placed on the student writers in our study will help us to teach the real "basics" more effectively to all students, including those labeled as "underprepared" or "basic writers."

I address several different audiences in this volume: composition specialists who design and teach first-year writing courses, faculty across the disciplines interested in improving student writing, and administrators engaged in revising general education and major programs. I have aimed for a concise, practical analysis, useful to a broad audience. I write at a time when academics in the increasingly sophisticated field of composition and rhetoric seem beset by doubts about the value of the work they have traditionally undertaken in first-year composition, writing-across-the-curriculum programs, and writing assessment.

Sharon Crowley (1991, 1998), Lil Brannon, David Jolliffe, Charles Schuster (as cited in Connors, 1996), and others have recently argued for the abolition of the nearly universal first-year composition requirement on the grounds that it cannot deliver the writing skills that students and faculty across the disciplines expect and it creates a ghetto of underpaid writing instructors. Writing-across-the-curriculum programs (WAC) have developed as a complement or alternative to first-year writing courses. Yet, here again, Barbara Walvoord (1996), writing on the 25th anniversary of WAC programs, notes "a pervasive sense of uncertainty" (p. 58). In her article, "The Future of WAC," she summarizes some of the "threats and enemies" noted by experienced WAC leaders, which include "counterproductive attitudes and assumptions about writing and learning in the university" and the "lack of an appropriate theoretical and research base" (p. 58).

While teachers and administrators struggle with these uncertainties within the field of composition and rhetoric, they are increasingly under pressure to assess and demonstrate student learning. But recent volumes on evaluation (Cooper & Odell, 1998), on portfolios (Yancey & Weiser, 1997), on grading (Allison, Bryant, & Hourigan, 1997), and on assessing writing-across-the-curriculum programs (Yancey & Huot, 1997), as well as any issue of the journal, *Assessing Writing,* provide evidence of how difficult it is to identify what makes writing good and what should count as appropriate development, either in the classroom or in larger institutional settings.

Within the composition establishment, unfortunately, there is little research tracing the development of college writers over the long term that might inform discussions of these complex questions: What is the role of first-year composition? How can faculty best assess and support the development of students' writing abilities across the curriculum? Marilyn Sternglass's *Time to Know Them* (1997) stands out as a notable exception, following a group of writers from their beginning composition courses and demonstrating their growth in writing and learning in their major areas of study. She analyzes teaching strategies that do or do not support this growth. She convincingly argues that one-time institutional assessments often fail to capture development that occurs slowly over time.

In this volume, I offer a longitudinal study of another group of students and the literacy environment they experienced in college. While the problem areas I have sketched are too complex to be considered in-depth in any single study, examining literacy in college from the students' perspective does offer new insights. My analysis of the data collected in this study supports a limited but still useful role for first-year composition, demonstrates how students do learn to write differently across the curriculum in ways that may or may not be recognized by faculty, and examines the teaching and learning practices that promote or constrain student development.

Based on what was learned from students in my study, I make general recommendations to support students' development as they take on new roles as writers, both in first-year writing courses and in more specialized academic majors. As the quote by developmental psychologist Urie Bronfenbrenner asserts at the beginning of this preface, it is the almost "magiclike power" of these changing roles and expectations that alters college writers' ways of thinking and acting. Some of the recommendations in this volume will be familiar to faculty already engaged in writing across the curriculum or in teaching strategies that promote active learning and critical thinking. However, I want to demonstrate how student data support these recommendations and elaborate on how they play out in practice, especially in the practices of students themselves.

Chapter 1 introduces the thesis that students in college do not necessarily learn to write "better," but that they learn to write differently—to produce new, more complicated forms addressing challenging topics with greater depth, complexity, and rhetorical sophistication. What are often called "writing assignments" in college are, in fact, complex "literacy tasks" calling for high-level reading, research, and critical analysis. Both composition teachers in first-year courses and faculty in other academic disciplines may underestimate the difficulty of such tasks, students' needs for repeated practice, and the ways in which expectations for literacy differ across disciplines, courses, and professors. This chapter briefly reviews research that supports this more complex view of literacy and examines studies of writing across the disciplines. Four profiles of students writing in different academic disciplines preview the variety and difficulty of the new roles and tasks students are asked to take on during their college years. The chapter establishes a cultural or environmental view of writing development drawing on the work of psychologists Lev Vygotsky (1978), Urie Bronfenbrenner (1979), Jerome Bruner (1986, 1996), and Michael Cole (1996). The conclusion offers a challenge to composition specialists to rethink the first-year composition course and their role as "writing missionaries" to other academic disciplines.

In chapter 2, I sketch the culture of the college and the students presented in this study, situating the literacy practices of students and faculty within a school context and previous research on the politics of literacy. In the chapter, I describe the longitudinal, portfolio-based assessment project that provided data for this study, review the qualitative methodology used to collect and analyze data, and consider both the ethical and practical problems of validly representing participants in a qualitative study, especially in terms of gender, class, and race. Chapter 2 introduces, with brief profiles, the additional students in the study with majors in the humanities, communication, science, social sciences, and business.

In chapter 3, I examine how students' experiences in their first two years of college shape their development as writers. I look closely at some of the specific writing environments students encounter and demonstrate the frequently painful process that students undergo as they attempt to meet the varying literacy expectations of different professors. Writing across the curriculum is a roller coaster with much writing in some semesters and little in others. In their introductory classes in general education, students especially value literacy projects that mark points of transition, "milestones" in their learning in which they are able to make connections between their writing and their own developing interests. Some of the best of these projects are supported by "hands-on" learning outside the classroom. First-year writing serves as a transition from students' previous writing experiences in high school to the demands of the new roles they will take on in college. In composition courses, students focus explicitly on their own literacy and develop new writing strategies as they are "forced" to change their "normal" ways of writing. In their general education courses, students have few opportunities to write in-depth or develop a particu-

lar type of writing over time. A four-semester Great Books Colloquium offers one opportunity for this kind of sustained growth,
though, as in first-year composition, the lessons learned do not necessarily carry over to writing in other disciplines.

Chapter 4 shows how students negotiate the writing demands
of their major disciplines and challenges again the fantasy that students should already know how to write for situations they have not
yet encountered. In this chapter, I examine how a variety of disciplines, some more than others, provide "scaffolding" to support students' new roles as writers. Through research and writing courses,
teacher and peer response, and "hands-on" experience, students
develop a better sense of "what the professor wants" and come to
explain some of these expectations as necessary, even useful, conventions of their academic fields. Students' performances as writers
are constrained as well as enabled by the circumstances of writing
for the college classroom. Composition specialists need to understand diverse writing environments from the participants' perspective, especially that of students. In this chapter, I demonstrate how
students' literacy development continues, though not always in linear and consistent ways apparent to individual faculty members in
single courses.

Chapter 5 contains a summary of study conclusions, focusing particularly on the role of first-year composition in writing development, supporting the usefulness of upper-level writing requirements, and arguing for a more contextualized view of writing
assessment. In the last section of this chapter, I propose recommendations for instruction across the curriculum, including taking
seriously students' questions about "what the professor wants," examining closely the literacy environments we coconstruct with students, and altering these environments as necessary to support development as students rehearse new roles as writers.

Acknowledgments

Although the conclusions and any errors in this study are my own, many people have contributed to this work. I especially appreciate the support of Don Thompson, academic dean of Seaver College, Pepperdine University, and cochair of the CD–ROM Student Portfolio Project. I want to thank Henry Gambill, research assistant for the project and now Seaver College director of assessment; the staff who developed our web site and downloaded the digital portfolios, especially Chuck Manning, Matt Daugherty, Steve Thompson, and Joseph DiIanni; and the student workers who patiently waded through files and phone calls, sharing their insights with us. I have benefited greatly from the ideas of Seaver College faculty members who participated in project workshops during summer 1995 and summer 1996, from work with my colleagues in composition and rhetoric at Pepperdine, and from ongoing discussions with members of the Los Angeles Composition/Literacy Study Group. Reviewers for Studies in Writing and Rhetoric and especially the series editor, Robert Brooke, generously made extensive comments that helped me shape my argument.

I also want to thank Louise Wetherbee Phelps, W. Ross Winterowd, Marilyn Cooper, and Michael Holzman who introduced me to developmental and cultural perspectives in the rhetoric, linguistics, and literature program at the University of Southern California. And, most of all, I want to thank the students in our study who were willing to share their college experience with me.

Rehearsing New Roles

1 / A Preview of Writing Development

> Our analysis alters the traditional view that at the moment a child assimilates the meaning of a word, or masters an operation such as addition or written language, her developmental processes are basically complete. In fact, they have only just begun at that moment.
>
> —Lev Vygotsky, *Mind in Society*

It was the kind of note all too familiar to writing center directors. Professor X in the business division had sent me a copy of a student paper, the printed text barely readable through the professor's copious corrections. Professor X complained that he had directed the student, Eric, to the writing center, but his final draft was still filled with errors and sometimes incoherent. Who had tutored this student? I did, I realized as I reviewed the paper. I remembered the assignment for a freshman seminar class, "Discuss the ethics of the ZZZZ Best case." (Despite a general shift in the academy to gender-neutral language, this required first-year introduction-to-college course is still called a *freshman* seminar.) Eric and I had spent half an hour trying to untangle information about the case—a complicated series of frauds perpetrated by an overly zealous young entrepreneur named Barry Minkow, who had turned a carpet-cleaning business into a financial empire built on other people's money. Minkow had fooled hundreds of investors and numerous accountants, so it is no wonder that Eric and I had some trouble following the ins and outs of his schemes. Eric's paper was still confusing when he had to rush off to his next class. He didn't have time to come back to the writing center but vowed to revise, at least to get his facts straight, before he turned his paper in to Professor X later in the day. His final draft, slightly rearranged, was not much better than his first.

I sympathized with Professor X, who assured me that Eric's

paper was not an exception, only the worst of a very bad set of essays, despite the fact that every student had been required to "stop by" the writing center. After I explained why I was unable to fix Eric's paper in half an hour, Professor X shifted the blame for Eric's poor performance to his high school teachers, saying it was a shame that these young people hadn't been taught to write *before* they got to college. I share Professor X's fantasy that someone somewhere could teach students to write once and for all, so that ever after one has only to say, "discuss romanticism, or stock market fluctuations, or world hunger, or the life cycle of tree frogs," and a stack of well-crafted, cogently argued, eminently readable essays would appear. But how close is that fantasy to the reality of how students develop as writers during their college years?

Writing Ability and Literacy Tasks

The 20 students in the study group we followed for four years would probably be judged to have been at least adequately prepared for college based on traditional measures such as high school GPA's, SAT/ACT scores, and the mostly "A" and "B" grades they earned in their first-year college courses. Yet these students often felt besieged by a barrage of disparate writing tasks in their first two years of college and needed continuing support and practice in their junior and senior years to develop proficiency in the specific genres of writing in their academic majors. They were unable to fulfill the fantasy that they should be able to write fluently on any topic and under any circumstances.

Much of the frustration experienced by students like Eric and their professors comes from a misunderstanding of what constitutes "writing" in college. Current theorists in composition, especially those who draw on postmodernist views of knowledge and discourse as socially constructed, challenge the notion of a stable, unified "writing ability" that can easily be measured by looking at isolated texts. They portray writers not as isolated individuals reaching within themselves to produce original writing but as more fluid selves pulling together bits and pieces of language to accomplish social and cultural goals. (See, for example, Bartholomae, 1985; Berlin, 1992; Carroll, 1997; Clifford & Schilb, 1994; Faigley, 1992; Harkin & Schilb, 1991; McLaren & Lankshear, 1993; Miller, 1991.)

From this perspective, Witte and Flach (1994) argue that "the advanced ability to communicate effectively" expected in college cannot be assessed apart from the contexts in which individuals use writing, speech, and other sign-systems to accomplish specific purposes. "Ability" is an abstract concept inferred from the individual's performance in specific situations, and our judgments of success or nonsuccess vary, according to the context in which communication occurs. Situations requiring advanced ability, as in college writing assignments, are often "messy," presenting ill-defined problems, and as Witte and Flach note,

> it is the ability to deal effectively and appropriately with the social messiness of text (broadly defined) production and use in naturally occurring situations and contexts that lies at the heart of our conceptualization of "advanced ability." (p. 226)

Myers (1996) calls this ability to use language and other sign-systems strategically "translation/critical literacy" as opposed to the "decoding/analytical literacy" that was emphasized in schools for most of the past century. He demonstrates how rapid changes in information technology, media, and the workplace require that students, citizens, and workers not only be able to decode and analyze texts but also to manage actively their own use of language, to match resources to problems, to shift between different modes of communication and sign-systems, and to understand differences in styles of discourse (pp. 285–288).

What are usually called "writing assignments" in college might more accurately be called "literacy tasks" because they require much more than the ability to construct correct sentences or compose neatly organized paragraphs with topic sentences. In order to complete these "writing assignments," students must, in fact, or-chestrate a complicated sequence of "literacy acts."

Eric, for example, in order to complete Professor X's rather vague and open-ended assignment, needed to locate relevant infor-mation about ZZZZ Best on the Internet and digital databases. He needed to read and understand the financial, legal, and ethical as-pects of the case and explain his understanding in a conventional academic essay form. And he needed to produce this revised and edited essay in one or two weeks. In this more complicated sense, Eric, a first-year student, does not "write" well enough for Professor X's class. It would be helpful to Eric and Professor X to rethink this supposedly basic writing assignment in terms of the more complex literacy tasks it involves. Projects calling for high levels of critical literacy in college typically require knowledge of research skills, ability to read complex texts, understanding of key disciplinary concepts, and strategies for synthesizing, analyzing, and respond-ing critically to new information, usually within a limited time frame.

The complexity and messiness of this critical literacy, with writing as only one component, makes it difficult to accurately as-sess a student's writing ability at any given point in the student's career and even harder to measure a student's "development" over several years. What is good writing by a first-year student; how will we define "better" four or five years later? Most writing programs have rubrics that outline criteria for judging writing in first-year classes, and these criteria are often taken to be general standards by which most student academic writing can be judged. While such rubrics can increase the reliability of judgments among trained readers, important in high-stakes exams and in grading by differ-ent teachers across many sections of the same course, they cannot, as this study will show, adequately account for the success or non-success of students as they go about their actual work as writers across the university. Any assessment of writing ability must exam-ine the interplay between the writer and the learning environment and take into account the writer's perception of the task, as well as the "objective" reality of the situation.

Examining Writing and Literacy Across Academic Disciplines

In order to more fully understand the complex literacy tasks required in college, we asked our 20 students to collect portfolios of their writing across a variety of disciplines, to complete regular self-assessments, and to participate in a series of focus groups and interviews about their academic work. Our data suggest that both composition faculty and professors of courses in disciplinary majors are likely to have distorted views of student literacy. The composition establishment tends to view writing through the wrong end of the telescope, focusing on forms of writing appropriate to first-year composition courses but often mistaking these forms for academic writing in general. In fact, composition specialists may be dismissive of discipline-specific genres that do not meet their own criteria for good writing. When I presented samples of advanced student writing in science and literature at a writing conference, samples that had been judged as very successful by the student writers and their professors, some writing teachers dismissed the science writing as lacking a sense of audience and voice, and others said that the literature essay was "too jargony." These teachers much preferred a pop-up book on insects, written by two biology students in the writing-across-the-curriculum course of another presenter, also a composition teacher. The pop-up book may be an excellent writing-to-learn activity, requiring biology students to explain their specialized knowledge in an entertaining way to a less knowledgeable audience; however, this type of assignment cannot replace the more difficult work in science and in literature of writing about specialized topics for more critical readers.

It is no wonder, then, that when our study students looked back on their first-year composition courses, their descriptions of their writing in these courses ranged from fun and creative to frustrating and random. For these students, first-year composition served primarily as a transition from high school—not the capstone of their K–12 literacy careers but an introduction to the more diverse ways of writing expected of prospective psychologists, scientists, philosophers, or business managers. While most students gave composition classes credit for promoting some general writing and research skills, all continued to learn new, more complex, and, often, quite different ways of writing in their major disciplines.

On the other hand, professors in major disciplinary courses may underestimate how different their expectations about writing are from those that students have already experienced and how much practice is needed to apply discipline specific concepts, knowledge, and conventions in writing. Because faculty across the disciplines tend to see writing as a unitary ability simply applied in a variety of different circumstances, they often focus their attention on the most obvious features of student writing—word choice, sentence structure, usage, punctuation—and, like Professor X, spend precious hours actually rewriting student work. Professors in major disciplinary courses who often assign only one or two pieces of writing a semester tend to miss the bigger picture of how student writing develops slowly over several years. These teachers may continue to mistake a one-time performance constrained by time and circumstance for an abstract quality called writing ability.

Unfortunately, few research studies have looked closely at how students actually negotiate the frustrations and successes of writing across disciplines over time. In a classic work from 1975, *The Development of Writing Abilities (11–18)*, James Britton and his co-authors, Burgess, Martin, McLeod, and Rosen, analyzed "2122 pieces of writing from sixty-five secondary schools by school students in the first, third, fifth and seventh years, drawn from all subjects of the curriculum where extensive writing was used" (p. 7). Rejecting previous methods of evaluating student writing, they developed a multidimensional model, demonstrating how the students' sense of audience and ability to employ different functions of writing developed over their secondary school years. Their conclusions were fresh at the time and highly relevant to future studies, including my own. First, development in secondary schools does not mean progress in a single kind of writing but in the ability to produce different kinds of writing successfully. Secondly, writing may actually become more difficult as writers increasingly recognize the need to address these different tasks at greater levels of complexity. And finally, various disciplines teach ways of writing that are not only different but, often, contradictory. Britton et al. summarize, "As for the student—if it is not always all cries and confusion, it is sometimes a bit like a tug of war" (p. 139).

More recent studies have closely analyzed this "tug of war" at the college level. Walvoord and McCarthy (1990) demonstrate the difficulties students encounter in four disciplinary courses in business, history, human sexuality, and biology and show how each course presents unique problems in constructing the audience and the self, stating a position, using discipline-based methods of support, and organizing and managing complexity. Anderson et al. with Susan Miller (1990) and Chiseri-Strater (1991) remind us how much student learning goes on independently, how students learn to play the game of school, and how a limited version of literacy may constrain rather than enhance development.

Writing in college is sometimes presented benignly as an invitation to students to join an ongoing conversation, a discourse community of scholars passionately and dispassionately searching for truth. However, examinations of academic discourse by writers like Linda Brodkey (1987), Patricia Bizzell (1992), and Marilyn Cooper (1986, 1990) reveal the complex web of social practices that shape what can and cannot be said. Historical, political, and economic forces influence the practices of writers in academic disciplines, and these social practices continue to evolve in ongoing interactions. How do students negotiate these unfamiliar practices? Within disciplines, experienced writers are themselves often unable to articulate exactly what they do. Research studies help to unravel the tacit processes by which not only texts but knowledge itself is produced. For example, studies by Geisler (1994), Haas (1994), Stockton (1995), and MacDonald (1994) look closely at reading and writing practices in philosophy, biology, history, literature, and psychology. Volumes edited by Jolliffe (1988) and Herrington and Moran (1992) collect additional studies that suggest how students become acculturated to the "ways of knowing" in various academic disciplines. Much of this research takes a pragmatic approach— look at how experts do literacy, look at how students do it, teach students to be more like experts. At the same time, acculturation is not a universal goal. Geisler (1994), writing about philosophy as a discipline, argues,

> But, as we have seen, academic expertise is a culture into which all students neither want nor need to enter. For this reason, we need to use the curriculum to find a way to interact with those who are different than us and intend to stay that way. A reconceptualized general education would acknowledge the difference between expert and amateur perspectives and give as much attention to educating the one as the other. (p. 255)

Sternglass's *Time to Know Them* (1997) is one of the few truly longitudinal studies that captures both the academic environments in which students write and, most importantly, their perception of this environment and demonstrates why composition specialists and faculty across the curriculum need to pay careful attention to both environment and perception if they want to understand and support student development. In the study reported on here, we attempt to understand another group of students in a different environment.

Profiles of Writing Development

The gap between faculty fantasies about writing and the reality of students struggling to make sense of academic literacy is best illustrated by actual portfolios of student work and the responses of teachers and students themselves to this work. The 20 different students have 20 different portfolios with characteristic strengths, weaknesses, and interests that reappear in their work over time. However, some general patterns do emerge. I would like to profile 4 of these students here to lay the groundwork for the claims I will develop in the next three chapters. These claims include:

- Writing assignments in college generally call for high levels of critical literacy, typically requiring skills in researching, reading complex texts, understanding of key disciplinary concepts, and strategies for synthesizing, analyzing, and responding critically to new information, usually within a limited time frame.
- Faculty are likely to underestimate how much writing tasks differ from course to course, from discipline to discipline, and from professor to professor.
- Lessons learned in first-year writing courses do not directly transfer to students' work in their major areas of study.
- Students who begin as fluent, effective writers generally continue to be successful, though their writing sometimes appears to be weaker when they encounter new and unfamiliar expectations.
- Students who demonstrate difficulty both in writing and learning content material, nonetheless, do come to better understand the genres and demands of their disciplines and show increasing (but not perfect) ability to write in these genres. Professors reading individual papers in upper-division courses are unlikely to observe this growth over time, and their comments reveal both their patient efforts to help students improve and their frustration that some of their junior and senior students "still can't write."
- Students' literacy develops *because* students must take on new and difficult roles that challenge their abilities as writers. In fact, student writing may sometimes need to get "worse" before it can get "better." Because many college writing tasks are essentially new to students, they will need repeated practice to become proficient.
- Comparing the writing of students across disciplines on standardized assessment tests cannot capture the diversity of their literacy experiences or their ability to use

literacy successfully in negotiating the demands of their major disciplines.

The four profiles of Sarah, Carolyn, Kristen, and Andrea illustrate the variety and complexity of literacy tasks that engage students across disciplines. These profiles demonstrate why it is not possible to design a one-size-fits-all writing curriculum that can prepare all students for writing situations they have not yet encountered. Instead, each of the four young women profiled in this chapter did develop new literacy skills to meet the demands of new roles she desired or was required to play.

Sarah: The Peculiar World of English Majors
Because writing in high school and college is taught most directly in literature and composition classes, students and faculty members may either consciously or unconsciously base many of their assumptions about "writing" on the kinds of writing typically produced in English courses. In reality, the literacy world of English majors is somewhat peculiar in that English majors, unlike students in other majors, continue from high school and throughout college to produce a similar genre of highly text-based, usually thesis-driven essays. Sarah, for example, an English major and philosophy minor, perfected this similar style of writing from her first year in a "Great Books" alternative to her first-year composition course to her senior honors seminar. Therefore, it is relatively easy to trace a consistent pattern of development from the first essays in her portfolio from her first year to the work she completed in her junior and senior years.

Sarah began her English studies in 5th grade in Eastern Europe and continued in an American 7th grade ESL class when her family immigrated to the United States. An avid reader from a literary family, she scored 620 on the SAT verbal in the 11th grade and graduated from high school in Arizona with a 4.00 GPA. She graduated from Pepperdine University with a GPA of 3.71, as well as more than $20,000 in financial-aid loans.

In September of 1994, during her first semester of college,

Sarah wrote an essay on "Fate vs. Free Will As Acted Out In the Iliad," which her teacher marked, "A," " <u>Very</u> well done—well argued & gracefully written." This essay began:

> The founding pillars of *The Iliad* constitute of [*sic*] a series of questions which Homer repeatedly rises [*sic*] as the plot unfolds. How far can an individual be held responsible for actions which are the result of some direct divine intervention? What is to be considered fate, and what free will? Is there in *The Iliad* any developed concept of free and responsible human deeds? As the epic poem is analyzed we can find enough examples to support and negate any answer we might consider true. Homer provides no concrete answers to such questions, but rather incites the reader to analyze own [*sic*] existence through the lens of the Greek and Trojan culture.

In four and a half pages, Sarah developed her thesis, citing evidence to support her analysis of the roles of fate and free will in *The Iliad*. She was especially good at dealing with these themes from several perspectives, considering complexity and ambiguity in the epic.

Almost two years later, Sarah still demonstrated a rather florid style and increasing sophistication as a literary critic. For modern drama, she wrote about Heiner Muller's play *Hamletmachine* in an essay she entitled "Shakespeare's Factory." It began:

> Toward the end of the twentieth century, Beckett got his foot in the door of a new era in literature, a period permeated by a post-Cartesian rationalism which adopted an avant-garde opposition to social and artistic conventions, or as it was more poetically phrased by Adorno and Horkheimer in *Dialectic of Enlightenment,* a gradual "disenchantment of the world". [*sic*] This period, shattered by an alarming obsession with "reality" and its "representation" became to be known as the postmodern period. "Meaning" ironically rediscovered itself in ways that revolutionized

theatre and blurred the well-defined spheres of what is perceived to be real in the world, and what is a mere artificial representation of it.

Sarah received an "A-/B+" on this essay. Perhaps because Sarah's writing was already fluent, her professor made few comments on the text and instead wrote a long and thoughtful response, urging Sarah to consider more deeply the political content of the play she was analyzing.

Sarah's portfolio contains many similar examples of successful writing on Milton's *Comus,* Conrad's *Heart of Darkness,* Mishima's *Sound of Waves,* Kingston's *The Woman Warrior,* and other writers and works. In addition, Sarah wrote her own poems and a play in a creative writing class. Only in her philosophy minor did she find that her usual style did not work quite so well. For example, although she received a "B" on her nine-page paper, "The Problematic Aspect of Descartes' Mind and Body Dualism," her professor marked and questioned word choices, sentences, and ideas in almost every paragraph, urging Sarah to write more simply, make more careful word choices, and develop more "direction" in her argument. Sarah recognized a difference in writing in English and writing in philosophy and explained that English allows more subjective interpretation. Philosophy for her required a more careful analysis of exactly what the writer is saying.

Sarah began as a successful academic writer and added to her repertoire as she progressed over four years. Because she practiced the genre of the critical/analytical essay throughout her college career, it is easy to find in her portfolio similar kinds of papers to compare as "pre-" and "post-" samples of the development of her writing. Faculty members across the disciplines may assume that this critical genre forms the basis for much of academic writing and advocate standardized testing in this general format to assure that students "can write" before they advance to new tasks. However, this may not be the type of writing that students outside of English majors actually want or need to be able to do in their own major areas of study.

Carolyn: Learning to Write as a Professional in Public Relations

Carolyn is a student I will return to frequently in this study. Although no one student can be typical of a whole group, Carolyn's SAT of 1060 and her high school GPA of 3.58 fall in the average range for her class. As a first-year student from Minnesota, Carolyn described herself as "well motivated." She originally considered majoring in biology but then chose public relations as better suited to her skills in working with people. Carolyn exemplifies how even students who would likely be judged well prepared for college still must develop new and unfamiliar forms of literacy.

Like Sarah in English, Carolyn as a communication major took her own writing seriously and was successful in her academic work from her first year. Yet much of Carolyn's work in her upper-division courses looked quite different from Sarah's and quite different from Carolyn's own work as a first-year student. It is difficult to make comparisons between Carolyn's essays in English I and II and her junior-year project in her public relations course, a twenty-six-page packet of materials promoting a charity fund-raising luncheon. Though this packet included several extended texts, they were in different genres. For example, an opening one-page statement of purpose began:

> Sleighbell is an annual luncheon put on by the Los Angeles Delta Delta Delta Fraternity Alumnae for the purpose of raising money for the fraternity's philanthropy: Children's Cancer Charities. All of the proceeds raised by Sleighbell will go to Children's Hospital Los Angeles Hematology-Oncology Research. Children's Hospital uses the money for research and also to pay for some of the procedures and treatments for children with cancer who's [sic] families need the financial help.

The packet also included explanations of mission, tactics, key messages, and logistics; a budget; an agenda for the luncheon; a speech to be given by guest speaker Elizabeth Dole (a Delta Delta Delta alumna); 8 press releases; and a publicity timeline. Each section was formatted appropriately using heads, subheads, and bullet points as needed. The style ranged from straightforward explanation to heartwarming appeal as in Dole's speech, which began:

> Mary is a beautiful three-year-old girl. She likes to play with dolls, sing "Patty Cake" and chase butterflies. Mary is not unlike other children her age in most respects. However, unlike other children Mary is not expected to see her fifth birthday. You see, Mary has been diagnosed with Leukemia.

Despite Carolyn's training in writing and editing as a future professional in public relations, her professor still found editing errors like "who's" instead of "whose" and made suggestions to improve her press releases. Yet this was a successful effort; Carolyn believed it represented her best work. As well as demonstrating writing appropriate for her purposes, it drew on her experience as a leader in her sorority and showed her ability to use a variety of public relations techniques in the service of a worthwhile cause.

Carolyn also did continue to write more traditional academic essays over her four years, especially in general education courses. In her major, her ten-page senior paper, "American Propaganda Against Japan Post Bombing at Pearl Harbor," was an analysis of "Techniques and Tactics Utilized by the *New York Times* and the *Los Angeles Times* on December 8, 1941." As a genre of writing, this essay was similar to a rhetorical analysis of a speech by President Clinton that Carolyn wrote in her first year. Carolyn received an "A-" on this eighteen-page research paper, an in-depth but somewhat loosely organized discussion of Clinton's oratorical background and his speech announcing the invasion of Haiti. She was proud of this essay, her first research paper in college. Her senior paper, however, was more tightly organized, more thoroughly researched with many more sources, and demonstrated a deeper understanding of persuasive strategies. This was a paper that Carolyn said she would not have been able to write as a first-year student, not because she lacked writing ability but because she did not have the necessary concepts and knowledge. Carolyn made similar comments about her senior thesis, a forty-page analysis of an advertising campaign at Northwest Airlines, where her father worked as a pilot.

Kristen: When the Going Gets Tough in Science
Kristen, a sports medicine major with SAT scores and a high school GPA similar to Carolyn's, also had the writing ability to complete successfully assignments in her general education and introductory courses but experienced difficulty when she faced new and more complex literacy tasks in her upper-division classes. One of her first research projects in college was a paper on scoliosis for her freshman seminar. She wrote:

> Scoliosis is a disease that affects many young people. It is prominent among young girls between the ages of 8–15 years but there have been cases of young boys with scoliosis. Scoliosis is defined as "a sideways curvature of the spine of 11 degrees or more" (3:26). The severity of scoliosis is measured in degrees of the curve. A mild curve is said to be 25 degrees and below, a moderate curve is 25–40 degrees, and a severe curve is 40 degrees and above. Doctors recommend treatments for cases of moderate or severe curves.

Kristen drew on eight sources for this five-page paper. It was essentially a report restating what she had learned. Although she had some difficulty citing sources correctly, the teacher marked the paper "90%," "Excellent bibliography. Overall a very good paper. Please see comments inside." Kristen did equally well in the winter of her sophomore year reporting on a research study on the physiology of exercise, for a sports medicine course. Her style had become more sophisticated; she could employ a more specialized vocabulary and concepts. This report began:

> The purpose of this study was to investigate the effect thirty hours of sleep loss would have on exercise performance and cardiorespiratory functions. Exercise perfor-

mance included maximal exercise performance and exercise endurance. Cardiorespiratory functions included blood gases, heart rate, minute ventilation, oxygen consumption, and carbon dioxide production rate. Also measured were plasma epinephrine and norepinephrine levels to assess the influence of sleep loss on baseline sympathetic activity. This study was necessary because college-age athletes do not always get enough sleep and jet lag is prevalent among athletes who travel long distances to perform.

Kristen's grade was 10 points out of 10 for this summary. She was equally successful on the 10 lab reports for this course, receiving only one grade lower than an 8 out of 10.

However, in the winter of her junior year, she was not as successful in her motor control and development course. Her professor made extensive corrections on her first lab report, an experiment in learning to juggle (see the following figure).

Use past tense!

The purpose of this experiment ~~is~~ *was* to critically examine the processes involved in learning.

It ~~is~~ hypothesized that the subject will (learn) to juggle throughout seven sessions of one-handed juggling.   *What does this mean?*

Center. underline needed.
No just bold!

(Results)

performance

The subject's ~~juggling~~ did improve as the study progressed from the first five

minute session through the seventh session of juggling. As seen in Figure 1, the subject's

average scores progressed in an upward trend. This shows that she began to improve ?   *?. Did you test for significance.*
slightly but did not improve (significantly) over the course of seven sessions. During   *What about session 2?*
the first few sessions, the subject's scores did not increase. The subject's fourth session   *When compared with session one?*
scores showed an improvement of about seventy percent. Also, the sixth session scores

showed an improvement of over sixty percent. *Compared with?*

Scores don't improve but performance does.

The professor's detailed comments and corrections continued for the entire five pages of the lab report. The tone of the comments and the frequent use of exclamation points suggest that the professor might have been somewhat exasperated by Kristen's inability to report data precisely, clearly, and in correct form. Kristen also had difficulty with basic concepts like performance, learning, improvement, and significance. She used these terms as they might apply in everyday speech, not as they should be applied in sports medicine. This project involved conducting an experiment, doing statistical analysis and graphing the results, reporting data, and explaining the conclusions that could be drawn. Kristen earned a "C" on this project, a low grade for her.

Yet, this was one of the projects Kristen chose to include in her digital portfolio. She explained that doing this first lab write-up was "a humbling experience" and that she did not do as well as she had hoped. Her paper was "ripped apart." However, it was helpful because she had a chance to improve. In this course, with a lab due almost every week, she could apply what she learned from each effort. By the end of the course, she received comments like "well-done" and "well written." The first lab was an important learning experience, and Kristen added that it was fun trying to learn to juggle with one hand.

Kristen's experience again challenges the fantasy that students can be taught to write at some particular point in their educational careers and ever after perform successfully regardless of context. I do not want to entirely discard the concept of "writing ability." Kristen clearly had skills and knowledge, both in writing and in her major field, that enabled her to produce a rough approximation of the lab report her professor required. Her previous experiences as a writer in general education and introductory major courses had helped build these abilities. However, in her motor control and development class, she needed to learn to write in a new situation for a new professional audience. We did not expect her to be able immediately to juggle with one hand, even though she undoubtedly had some experience throwing and catching balls. She needed feedback and practice to become proficient in juggling and in writing lab reports.

Andrea: Learning the Hard Way in Political Science

Andrea graduated from a public "magnet" high school in Los Angeles that emphasized math and science. Angela's father, who was an airplane technician, and her mother, a medical assistant, were working in Saudi Arabia at the time of our study. Although Andrea had a 530 SAT verbal score and a high school GPA of 3.69, she struggled to earn "C's" and "B's" in her political science and economics courses.

Andrea recalled her frustration in her first year when she was asked by her freshman seminar teacher to investigate the history of her African American family and integrate that history with library resources. Although the paper made interesting reading and she received a "B" on it, Andrea objected, "It literally takes people years to find out who they're related to, and he wanted us to do all that in one semester, and I thought that was literally impossible, and so I wasn't satisfied with the information I came up with." She did, however, locate ten sources and relate them to a family story. For example, after explaining the system of sharecropping, she wrote:

> Sharecroppers were forced to live in run-down shacks or cabins. Most of them were built out of sight because they were an eye sore to the white people. After Negroes became free, most of them traveled to the north, the land of opportunity. Some families willingly split apart and others traveled together to the north. Some families didn't want the city atmosphere and preferred the rural setting (Cole 156). Other families believed in superstition and that something bad will happen if they fled to the city (Cole 156).
>
> Along with some other families, my ancestors migrated from Pittsylvania county to Halifax county. There were various reasons why people migrated to different counties. The owners of the land sold their portion of the land and were forced to move to another county.

Despite some of her difficulties with this assignment, Andrea's writing was certainly adequate for this freshman seminar class. Her professor responded to her family story, commended her list of sources, and credited the paper with 45 points out of 50.

However, by winter 1996, her sophomore year, much more was required in her African political thought course. There were more than 55 comments, everything from one-word corrections to probing questions, on Andrea's eight-page paper, "Progress Within the Supreme Court." Although the professor in an endnote gave the paper a "B," he wrote:

+ good research but your arguments were hampered by grammatical and stylistic weaknesses.
+ There are a number of questions raised by this paper that you have not answered. (i.e.) What are the essential criticisms of the Court as a "friend" to Blacks viz. a viz. [sic] their inability to garner support in the Congress or executive branch?
+ What was Earl Warren's agenda in helping Blacks gain civil rights?
+ Your paper never makes an emerging point or theme.
+ Do you think that progress is occurring even in light of Shaw v. Reno 1993 & the recent anti-affirmative action cases in Texas? Univ. of California?
− spelling
− sentence structure needs development. Have your papers proof read [sic] before submission.

These were very similar to the comments of another professor in American foreign policy the previous semester and to the comments of her professor in jurisprudence, which she was also taking in winter 1996. By the fall of 1996, her junior year, Andrea was more proficient in writing legal briefs, especially because she had the opportunity to do three briefs in constitutional law, which earned a "B/B-," "A/A-," and "B/B+." Interestingly, in her "A" paper, Andrea took up the Shaw v. Reno case mentioned by her African political thought professor. After seventeen pages discussing background information and judicial opinion in the case, Andrea explained her opinion:

The Supreme Court's decision in this case deviated from the usual harm requirement in gerrymandering cases. The court held that designing legislative districts to increase minority representation may violate the equal protection rights of all voters. The Court reasoned that irregularly shaped districting plans may violate all voters equal protection rights because such plans reinforce harmful racial stereotypes. Because of this case, the standard will change in which a petitioner must satisfy to prove that a reapportinoment [sic] plan is violating the Equal Protection Clause.

The Shaw decision shows evidence that because the Supreme Court majority is adverse to affirmative action, our nation's advancement toward increasing minority membership in government has been severely threatened. Unfortunately, the Court chose to engage in an attack on the Voting Rights Act.

In the following paragraph, Andrea continued to explain why she disagreed with the Shaw decision. Clearly, her experience in the jurisprudence and African political thought courses helped her develop concepts, content knowledge, and ways of writing that she applied in this paper. She also was more willing to invest effort in a topic that interested her.

Yet, Andrea's writing, like that of many students, tended to be uneven. Here is her answer, written during the final semester of her senior year, to a humanities exam question about the romantic hero:

The idea of a romantic hero was portrayed through music, art, and literature. The romantic hero was a super human who had the ability to persevere for the betterment of mankind. In Wagner's, Nieblung, Siegfried was a romantic hero because he wanted to obtain knowledge and power from a golden ring, but he was betrayed and killed. Romantic heroes were looked upon as god-like or they wanted to obtain a special ability. In Lord Byron's Don

Juan, Don Juan was lover with insatiable needs. Beethoven viewed himself as a romantic hero because he was a brilliant musician, yet he was going deaf. In the "Wrath of Medusa" [sic] by William Turner [sic], Turner showed the agony in which 11 men persevered after being on a raft for 2 weeks without food or water.

On another answer from the same exam, the professor commented that Andrea should "not just memorize points" but "must connect them." Her exam answers in public policy warranted similar comments. On these essay exams, it is difficult to separate the quality of writing from the knowledge of subject matter. Andrea could write well enough to explain Shaw v. Reno, but in this required general education course that she had put off taking, she clearly did not know, and perhaps did not care, much about romantic heroes. Her final papers in her major, during this semester, were also not her best efforts. A book review in criminology basically summarized Mikal Gilmore's Shot in the Heart, and her report of a service project at a juvenile detention camp earned only a "C" because she consulted no new sources beyond Gilmore. Her final paper in a course on third world and developing countries was an extremely detailed fourteen-page single-spaced report on Ethiopia, but it included little analysis and seemed to be almost entirely drawn from one U.S. government publication, Ethiopia: A Country Study, and the CIA web site.

Did Andrea's writing get "worse" in her senior year? It may be that her final semester was partly a case of "senioritis." Being strategic about how she invested her time, she did just enough to maintain her 3.0 GPA. Would she be able to write well enough to succeed in her goal of attending law school? Certainly, she learned new content and new ways of writing that she did not know as a first-year student. She said she thought that she had improved at writing in her major. She characterized this writing as being based on facts with no "frills." But, perhaps, she misinterpreted. In fact, her writing could use more "frills"—more analysis, more development, more argument. I suspect that if she does go to law school, her experience there might be similar to her experience at Pepperdine. As she said, "It's bad that you have to learn the hard way," learning as you go, not knowing it all before you start. And yet, that is the way many literacy tasks are learned. We learn as the need arises and, often, just enough to meet our personal and professional requirements. Reviewing Andrea's portfolio, it's easy to focus on what she did not do and to overlook all she learned, especially in following her own interests in law, civil rights, and African American studies. Two internships in Washington, D.C., gave her practical experience in addition to her classroom learning. Law school would be a new environment and present new writing challenges, but Andrea developed enough knowledge and skills to take her next steps, and she demonstrated a strong drive to learn what she wanted to know.

A Cultural/Environmental View of Development

A preliminary analysis of students' portfolios of writing and their reflections on that writing indicates that our study group did learn to write differently in college and to write better in the sense of producing new, more complicated texts, addressing challenging topics with greater depth and complexity. How can we begin to describe, account for, and support this development? A cultural or environmental view of development explains the almost "magic-like" power of new environments and new roles to "alter how a person is treated, how she acts, what she does, and thereby even what she thinks and feels" (Bronfenbrenner, 1979, p. 6). It is this perspective on development that underlies my preliminary analysis here and the more detailed analysis in the following chapters.

The cultural view of development is outlined by psychologist Urie Bronfenbrenner in his 1979 book, *The Ecology of Human Development*, and further developed by Jerome Bruner (1986, 1996), Michael Cole (1996), and others. Based on the work of earlier developmental psychologists, especially Lev Vygotsky (1978 ed.), Bronfenbrenner defines development as "the person's evolving conception of the ecological environment, and his relation to it, as well as the person's growing capacity to discover, sustain, or alter its properties" (p. 9). Bronfenbrenner's definition challenges us to re-think the notion of development as simply getting better at the same task over a period of time. The college students in my study, as in Britton et al. (1975), did not necessarily get better at some predetermined type of academic writing. Instead, they acquired a "more extended differentiated, and valid conception of the eco-logical environment" (Bronfenbrenner, 1979, p. 27). In students' own words, they became better at figuring out "what the professor wants." These successful students learned to accommodate the of-ten unarticulated expectations of their professor readers, to imitate disciplinary discourse, and, as juniors and seniors, to write in forms more diverse and complex than those they could produce when they entered college.

This development, however, was neither constant nor linear. Michael Cole (1996), perhaps best known to composition special-ists for his work with Sylvia Scribner, *The Psychology of Literacy* (1981), has more recently applied the perspective of cultural psy-chology to studying children and reading. He notes, "Long-term in-volvement with a single group of children forces the analyst to recognize the individuality of each child and the difficulty of deter-mining an analytic origin, a 'first' from which it is possible to de-duce conclusions logically" (p. 346). He explains how each child exhibits individual patterns of strengths and weaknesses and nego-tiates ways to minimize disadvantages in reading. There is not a single, unitary theory to predict how the child will handle tasks in the environment.

Bronfenbrenner (1979) emphasizes that development, instead of being a continuous process, takes place during periods of transi-tion. For students, each semester in college involves various types of transitions, and each course, each professor, each task repre-sents a more or less different ecological environment. Transitions promote development because "they almost invariably involve a change in *role,* that is, in the expectations for behavior associated with particular positions in society" (p. 6). The variety of these ex-pectations is often underestimated by faculty who again fanta-size writing as a stable skill that can simply be applied in different circumstances rather than as a complex set of abilities developing unevenly through many periods of transition requiring a variety of different roles.

However, students are far from helpless subjects of these transitional environments. As Cole (1996) points out, "individuals are active agents in their own development but do not act in settings entirely of their own choosing" (p. 104). Within these settings, Bronfenbrenner (1979) stresses that "what matters for behavior and development is the environment as it is *perceived* rather than as it may exist in 'objective' reality" (p. 4). Students are actively involved in figuring out "what the professor wants" and how they, as young adults, can accomplish their own goals within the college environment. Students employ literacy strategically as they find their own ways through the curriculum articulated by faculty. As other researchers have noted, this "experienced curriculum" is often at odds with the official curriculum described by faculty (Yancey, 1997). Faculty expectations for student writing in first-year composition and courses across the curriculum are often quite at odds with the perceptions of the students in my study who see writing as just one small part of their overall college experience. Problems that puzzle faculty, such as how to give feedback, how to handle errors, and how to grade student work, are highly dependent on students' own perceptions of feedback, errors, and grades and highly influenced by other factors in the college environment, especially time constraints.

Cole (1996) emphasizes that from the perspective of cultural psychology "mind emerges in the *joint* mediated activity of people. Mind, then, is in an important sense, 'co-constructed' and distributed" (p. 104). Jerome Bruner (1996) describes the ideal environment promoting learning as a "mutual community," which "models ways of doing or knowing, provides opportunities for emulation, offers running commentary, provides 'scaffolding' for novices, and even provides a good context for teaching deliberately" (p. 21). Within this environment, Bruner argues, "Achieving skill and accumulating knowledge are not enough. The learner can be helped to achieve full mastery by reflecting as well upon how she is going about her job and how her approach can be improved" (p. 64). Dialogue between the learner and more proficient members of the learning community focuses not only on cognitive tasks, how to do the job at hand, but also creates metacognitive awareness. What processes are involved and how might they be applied in new settings?

How do the knowledge and skills of the community become part of the individual's development? Vygotsky's (1978 ed.) concept of the "zone of proximal development" connects learner and community. Writing in the early decades of the twentieth century, Vygotsky proposed the counterintuitive argument that the developmental level of a child should not be judged on what the child can do independently but by *"the level of potential development as determined through problem solving under adult guidance or in collaboration with more capable peers"* (p. 86). He labels as the "zone of proximal development" the gap between the child's level of independent problem solving and the potential level of problem solving with help. Vygotsky demonstrates that the independent level only "defines functions that have already matured, that is, the end products of development" (p. 86). On the other hand, "the zone of proximal development defines those functions that have not yet matured but are in the process of maturation, functions that will mature tomorrow but are currently in an embryonic state" (p. 86). In a maxim that summarizes his point, Vygotsky states "what a child can do with assistance today she will be able to do by herself tomorrow" (p. 87).

Learning and development then take place in this zone of proximal development. If learners merely repeat tasks at which they are already proficient, no development occurs. In addition, as Vygotsky points out, development is also constrained when experienced practitioners within the learning community are unwilling or unable to help learners solve difficult problems. This failure either to present new problems or to provide assistance in problem solving "limits the intellectual development of many students; their capabilities are viewed as biologically determined rather than socially facilitated" (p. 126).

Challenging Faculty Fantasies About Writing

The cultural or environmental view of development again challenges faculty fantasies about writing. It challenges the notion that writing is a natural talent that cannot be taught. Instead, a cultural perspective directs our attention to the fact that writing is always learned in communities that contain both written texts and more experienced practitioners, the kinds of communities we would expect to find on college campuses. A developmental perspective also challenges the beliefs that students ought to know "how to write" before they get to college and that providing assistance amounts to what one professor I have worked with has called unnecessary hand-holding. In these beliefs, college faculty underestimate how writing in college calls for new forms of problem solving and new levels of development.

The study I present here attempts to dispel myths about writing and describe the ways in which college can function as a learning community, a supportive environment for the development of "translation/critical literacy" (Myers, 1996), "the advanced ability to communicate" (Witte & Flach, 1994). Further, our study students demonstrate that even when support is weak and inconsistent, student writers struggle to make sense of their own writing and become more rhetorically sophisticated, perhaps *because* they must often find their own ways, with little direct instruction, through changing contexts for writing.

This study seeks to fill the gap between the perception that students "can't write" and the reality that the thousands of students who earn undergraduate degrees each year are apparently able to "write" well enough to satisfy the requirements of their various academic programs. This study began, for me, with a number of simple observations familiar to writing teachers—that some students who cannot pass composition courses or exit exams in writing seem to do just fine in their other courses and, conversely, some students who do just fine in composition can't satisfy Professor X's requirements. Obviously, different environments require different kinds of writing. Although composition scholars reject narrow, basic skills definitions of writing, their own views of "academic writing" or "critical literacy" may be limited by their specific classroom contexts. What individual teachers identify as student resistance to meeting their idealized version of "good writing" or "critical thinking" can represent students' quite reasonable efforts to sort through multiple and, often, conflicting demands on their time and energy, hearts and minds. As other researchers have noted, the students' "experienced curriculum" is often at odds with the official curriculum described by faculty (Yancey, 1997). Students who move from course to course, from teacher to teacher, from one discipline to another, often have a broader view of writing in college than the faculty does, and this study is from their perspective.

My analysis challenges the myth that writing is a stable, unitary skill that can be learned once and then simply applied in new circumstances. It shows that the problems students face in writing in college are not primarily grammatical. Instead, our study students demonstrate that even writers who enter college proficient in constructing simple reports or arguments will struggle with tasks that require more complex analysis and methods of presentation. However, it is precisely in struggling with these challenging tasks that they develop new skills. Teachers and, later, employers can support novice writers in these periods of transition as writers work out their own strategies for learning in new roles.

An Admonition, a Dispensation, and a Challenge

The next four chapters will consider in more detail what we can learn from the study students about their development as writers and the role of faculty in supporting this development. However, a superficial overview already suggests the range of literacy tasks students complete in college and the variety in their preparation to take on these tasks. This overview prompts two observations.

First, from a personal perspective as a teacher of composition and a writing program administrator, I find, in students' portfolios of work collected over four years and in students' reflections on this work, both an admonition and a dispensation. The admonition is to take the work of teaching "writing" seriously in first-year composition; the dispensation is not to take it too seriously. A first-year composition course can serve students by helping them make connections between what they have already learned about writing in their K–12 education and ways they might learn to write differently both in the academy and as citizens of the larger society. On the other hand, first-year composition cannot succeed as a course that will teach students how to write for contexts they have not yet encountered. A one-semester writing course is best viewed as just one step in a long process of development that extends from children's first encounters with literacy on through their adult lives. For students, this step, the first-year composition course, can support their transition as writers from high school to college, but, it is, nonetheless, only one step, a step examined more closely in chapter 3.

Secondly, as a former writing center director and composition specialist responsible for working with faculty across disciplines, I find a challenge in what I have learned from students. Composition theory and pedagogy does not qualify me to preach one, true gospel of literacy or cast out of the congregation of good teachers those, like Professor X, who just do not seem to "get it." Segal, Pare, Brent, and Vipond (1998) suggest in their article, "The Researcher as Missionary: Problems with Rhetorical Reform in the Disciplines," that playing the missionary role is problematic, and rhetoricians instead ought to "gain knowledge slowly and respectfully, ideally with the collaboration or cooperation of the members of the community being studied," while concentrating "on problems that the practitioners recognize as significant within their own frame of reference" (pp. 84–85). They further admonish, "Don't expect to use what you know to save anyone" (p. 87). The challenge is to apprehend the powerful environmental forces that shape the literacy rituals and conventions of other folks. Students can be our best informants as each new recruit enters college and views with fresh eyes the rites of writing in the academy.

In chapter 2, I examine the cultural context and methodology of this study and briefly introduce the additional students in the study. Chapter 3 contains an analysis of student writing in general education and in first-year composition courses. Chapter 4 provides descriptions of students as they encounter the challenges of writing in their major areas of study.

2 / Studying College Writers: Context and Methods

Mike Rose, in "The Language of Exclusion," describes long standing laments in American colleges about students' lack of skills; indeed, such complaints were found at Harvard in the 1870s.
——Lynn Troyka, "Defining Basic Writing in Context"

Marilyn Sternglass (1997), who studied students labeled basic writers at City College in New York, calls for in-depth studies of students in many different contexts if we truly want to understand the development of literacy in college. Pepperdine University, on a hilltop overlooking the Pacific in Malibu, California, is about as far as you can get from City College and still be in the continental United States. Though Pepperdine students might sometimes be stereotyped as rich kids and surfers, they, in fact, come from a wide variety of backgrounds. However, most would identify themselves as middle to upper class, and they fit the profile of "traditional" college students, 18–22 years old and going to school full-time (although they may also be working and accumulating substantial loans). And yet, even these relatively advantaged students struggle with the advanced literacy tasks of college and, perhaps paradoxically, through that struggle become more competent writers. In the process, they often hide their confusion, boredom, anger—emotions they fear will jeopardize their chances for good grades and continuing success. And as at Harvard in the 1870s, as noted in the quote at the beginning of this chapter, so too do professors at Pepperdine University now lament students' lack of writing skills.

29

Writing and Literacy in a Cultural Context

The School Culture

Lynn Troyka shows in her classic essay, "Defining Basic Writing in Context" (1987), that judgments about who is prepared or underprepared for college level work are relative to the institutions and individuals making the judgment. An adequately prepared student at City College might be underprepared at Yale, and the literacy tasks expected of the undergraduate might vary as well. John Alberti in a more recent essay, "Returning to Class: Creating Opportunities for Multicultural Reform at Majority Second-Tier Schools" (2001), argues that too many academic discussions of issues, such as admissions standards, skills assessment, and general education reform, focus either on major research universities like Stanford and Berkeley or on high-profile cases such as the decision to remove "developmental" English and math courses from the open-admissions City University of New York. Alberti, who teaches at Northern Kentucky University, argues for a more fine-grained analysis of "place" in such discussions, giving more recognition to a wider variety of institutions where the majority of postsecondary students are educated.

The place of Pepperdine University and the kinds of literacy students practice there is in a somewhat ambiguous position along the continuum from elite research universities and selective liberal arts colleges to Alberti's second-tier, regional four- and two-year schools and for-profit institutions like the University of Phoenix. Founded in 1937 by George Pepperdine, who started a small mail-order business in auto parts and built it into the Western Auto Supply company, Pepperdine College was located near downtown Los Angeles until 1972 when the school moved to 830 acres of donated property in Malibu, California. At that time, the institution, begun by George Pepperdine as a small Christian college affiliated with the Churches of Christ, embarked on an ambitious program of expansion, leaving behind its urban origins.

Today, like many other institutions, Pepperdine University is something of a hybrid, and its conflicting goals are reflected in the literacy practices of students and faculty. The undergraduate school, Seaver College, which is focused on in this study, has sometimes been described by faculty as a preprofessional school masquerading as a liberal arts college. Although the university as a whole enrolls approximately 7800 full-time and part-time students, the undergraduate college is small, only 2700 students. The students at Seaver College are required to complete a fairly traditional core of 65 units of general education courses, about half the total units required for graduation, but the majority of students major in career-oriented programs in either business—with degrees in accounting, business administration, and international business—or in communication—with degrees in advertising, journalism, public relations, telecommunications, intercultural and organizational communication, and speech. Other career-oriented programs that are popular with students include teacher education, which offers an undergraduate teaching-credential program, nutrition, sports medicine, physical education, computer science, and, in the land of show business, theater and music. Student peer-advisors during orientation tell new students to sign up for general education courses as soon as possible and "get them out of the way," so they can move on to the important courses in their majors. Like undergraduates at other institutions, our students are understandably impatient when course work seems to have little relationship to their personal or career goals.

In addition to the tension between liberal arts and career education, several other conflicting institutional goals also cause frustration for students. Seaver College charges a very high tuition, over $24,000 a year but also gives about 70% of students financial aid in order to attract high-success high school students, outstanding athletes, members of the school-affiliated Churches of Christ, and diversity in the student body. Students and parents expect continuing academic success in return for the sacrifices necessary to support a student, even one with a financial-aid package, at an expensive school. Recruiting for diversity itself comes in conflict with the conservative, mostly white, Christian culture of a campus located in a notoriously expensive retreat from urban Los Angeles.

In the entering class that included our study students, 71% of the students identified themselves as White, 4% Black, 9% Hispanic, 8% Asian, 1% American Indian, and 7% as other or unknown. Of our total student body, more than 7% are international students, many of whom are from Muslim, Hindu, Buddhist, and other religious traditions. These international students are generally from wealthy families who can afford to pay full tuition for an American education in relatively protected surroundings. Though some efforts are made to recruit a more diverse student population, not all students feel welcome or at home on a still predominantly White campus.

Literacy in this academic environment works two ways, as it does in many American universities. On the one hand, it draws on a belletristic, liberal arts tradition that seeks to transmit cultural knowledge as cultural capital to the children of the middle and upper classes, though whose culture is transmitted is often hotly contested. On the other hand, literacy education also looks toward producing skilled workers for business and the professions and, in its most ideal iteration, knowledgeable citizens in a participatory democracy, two strong traditions in American postsecondary education. It is into this hybrid environment that, in 1994, our study students entered college as hopeful first-year students ready to start the next phase of their literacy education.

Background of the Study

In 1994, the General Education Committee at Seaver College received modest funding from the university to study a randomly selected sample of 46 incoming first-year students in order to assess student learning in our general education core curriculum. These students were to receive a unit of credit per year that they spent in the study and a small stipend for collecting syllabi, papers, exams and other written work from all their classes, for participating in interviews and focus groups, for completing assessment questionnaires, and, we argued to justify the unit of credit, for studying their own learning. Of our initial cohort of 46, about 30 students provided substantial data for the project, and 20 completed the four-year study, reviewing their portfolios in their senior year and participating in exit interviews.

The General Education Committee at Pepperdine was dissatisfied with previous attempts at curriculum evaluation that focused on student and faculty ratings of courses and on faculty syllabi indicating what faculty were teaching but not necessarily what students were learning. After reviewing projects at other institutions, particularly a large scale portfolio project at Miami University of Ohio and assessment seminars at Harvard University, the committee decided that a new study needed to include multiple sources of information, to be longitudinal, and, if findings were to have any credibility, to involve faculty across the disciplines.

The codirector of the assessment project, Don Thompson, a mathematician and now academic dean of Seaver, and I began to meet with students in a cluttered office in a corner of the library. We videotaped focus groups in which students discussed their initial experiences of college life and regularly collected from students either the originals or copies of all their written work (except course notes). At the end of each semester, students came to our office to update logs cataloging their work and to complete written self-assessments commenting on successful and unsuccessful learning experiences for each semester. Near the end of each year, writing center peer-tutors who had been trained to conduct interviews asked students to explain how and why they felt they had changed in 15 different areas ranging from involvement in service activities and interest in other cultures to mathematical/quantitative and communication skills. Interviewer notes and the taped interviews were added to each student's comprehensive portfolio. Though writing was not the only focus of the portfolio project, it was, of course, my primary interest, and as students discussed their written work, it became clear that writing played a central role in shaping and documenting their development as learners.

The original goal of the assessment project, to develop a comprehensive assessment of general education courses, was perhaps overly ambitious, considering the voluminous and "messy" nature of portfolio data. Nonetheless, small groups of faculty did meet in summer 1995 and 1996 to examine how general education courses addressed three areas: critical thinking, writing, and moral and ethical development, an especially important concern at a Christian university. Findings from the summer seminars fed into subsequent faculty workshops and ongoing discussions of general education reform.

Don Thompson, trying to reduce the general "messiness" of portfolio data, began experimenting with ways to have student materials scanned and stored on CD–ROM disks and officially dubbed our study the CD–ROM Portfolio Assessment Project. In fact, as the project evolved, web technology became more flexible, and in their senior year, the 20 students who completed the study selected representative samples of their work to create digital portfolios on individual web pages. Appendix A includes additional information about what is now called the Digital Portfolio Assessment Project (DPAP) at Pepperdine University, and the web address of our assessment office which houses the project. Although individual student portfolios are password protected to maintain student privacy, researchers may contact the assessment office through the web site to request access to view student portfolios.

Representing Our Students

I came to know the students in our study in interviews and meetings over four years. On a small campus, our paths crossed in classes and in the writing center. One of the study students worked in our project office, two others spent a semester studying abroad with me in Florence, Italy. Our final group of 20 students represented five of the seven academic divisions at Seaver College. Though there were no religion or fine arts majors, one student was a minor in religion, two had minors in art, and one in music. Our study group also represented a range of SAT scores and high school grade point averages typical of their entering class at Pepperdine. The mean SAT of the class of 1998 when they entered Pepperdine in 1994 was 1128; their mean high school GPA was 3.36. The SAT scores of our study group ranged from 830 to 1240, with 5 students scoring below 1000 and 3 students scoring above 1200. The high school GPA's of our study group ranged from 2.74 to 4.00, with 6 earning below a 3.0 and 5 earning above a 3.5. The final Pepperdine cumulative GPA's of the study group ranged from 2.2 to 3.8, a few points lower than their high school GPA's, but, again, with 6 students earning below a 3.0 and 5 students earning above a 3.5. A chart listing students' names (which have been changed to provide anonymity), majors, SAT and ACT scores, GPA's, and ethnicity is included in Appendix B.

We have not done a formal, follow-up study on the students who were in our original group of 46 but did not continue with the project. Our original group was a random sample of two students from each freshman seminar class in the fall of 1994. A computer-generated list of names included 36 women and only 10 men. We went ahead with this group even though it did not reflect the actual ratio of 59% women to 41% men on our campus. In the final group of 20, there were 16 women and 4 men. Of the 26 students who did not complete the project, we know that more than half, 14, did not continue at Pepperdine, and many of these transferred to other universities. We have partial data on most of the remaining students who stayed at Pepperdine but did not continue to participate in the project. Generally, these students reported that they were too busy or found it too burdensome to collect and turn in materials and come to interviews. The 20 students who completed the study reported that they liked being asked about their experience and having an impact on education at Pepperdine. They enjoyed being part of a special group. They also felt rewarded by having a record of their college experience and the tangible product of personal portfolios to represent their work. During their senior year, students chose from their comprehensive portfolios, collected over four years, anywhere from four to over ten pieces of work especially representative of their learning in college. These works were scanned to create a web-based digital portfolio for each student.

To represent participants in a qualitative research project is an endeavor fraught with opportunities for misrepresentation, a topic explored in-depth in a volume edited by Mortensen and Kirsch (1996), *Ethics and Representation in Qualitative Studies of Literacy.*

This is especially true when subjects in a study are particularly categorized as "other" on the basis of class, gender, race and ethnicity, sexual orientation, disability, et cetera. And yet, to erase these politically charged "differences" risks erasing socially and personally important parts of the subjects' experience. Nonetheless, I hesitated in this study based on a small sample of students to generalize about the effects of "difference," unless students self-identified themselves and pointed to the significance of such categories. Brenda Brueggemann (1996) in an essay in the Mortensen and Kirsch volume explains why she also avoids such generalizations in reporting on her research.

> For if there is but one thing I have learned well from my experiences tutoring and researching deaf students at Gallaudet it is that the diversity of their audiological, educational, family, linguistic, and cultural backgrounds makes characterizing a "representative" profile of such a student virtually impossible: there is simply no way to sum up what literacy skills might be expected from such students by the time they reach college-level course work. (p. 29)

Similarly, I resist making any of our study students representative of an essentialized "other."

However, this position causes particular problems describing students at Pepperdine, where most students see themselves as "mainstream" and many are politically conservative. The majority of European American students tend not to view their own "Whiteness" as a significant racial category and are reluctant to identify social class as a factor influencing their experience. In addition, even though there were 36 women and 10 men in our initial study group and 16 women and only 4 men in our final group of 20, these young, successful students seemed relatively unaware of how gender differences might have affected them in the classroom or as writers. On the other hand, a student who had immigrated with her family to the United States from Pakistan explained how she filtered much of her learning through her own cultural perspective. A shy, quiet, young White woman, Jeanette, majoring in accounting, could not find a comfortable role as an independent woman in college and went home every weekend to suburban Orange County where she worked at Disneyland. Most significantly, the two African American women in our study were keenly aware of "difference," and they explicitly connected race to some of the problems that they identified with their teachers, their writing, and their experiences on a mostly White campus.

In this study, while I must generalize to make sense of the data, I try to stay close to the voices of the study students, even at the risk of glossing over gender and racial or ethnic differences and appearing, perhaps, to single out the "difference" of African American students while ignoring the "Whiteness" of the majority. A saving grace, I hope, is that this first portfolio study did effectively highlight the overall lack of cultural awareness on our campus. With a grant from the James Irvine Foundation, another cohort of students is now being studied specifically to examine their perspectives on cultural diversity in more detail, and multiple programs are under way to attempt to diversify our campus through faculty development, cocurricular activities, curricular reform, and student and faculty recruitment. But that is the subject for another volume.

For the study presented here, I would not want to pretend that our small study group is somehow representative of the experience of college students in general. I leave it to readers to decide if the profiles of literacy I offer seem to fit at least some students at a variety of postsecondary institutions. As I noted at the beginning of this chapter, despite a range of family backgrounds, all of the students in this study would be likely to identify themselves as middle to upper class, and certainly as "non-poor." Our students attended college in pleasant surroundings with well-equipped classrooms and generally easy access to their teachers and were successful in graduating with bachelors' degrees. They studied writing in first-year classes limited to 18 students, unlike their peers at local community colleges who are often enrolled in writing classes with as many as 39 other students, with the presumption that many students will drop out.

Although our students may choose to be unaware of or to deny the effects of social class, their family backgrounds have, of course, shaped their access to educational opportunities, their literacy aspirations, and their literacy experiences. Elspeth Stuckey (1991), a passionate teacher who worked with me in an adult literacy program sponsored by the University of Southern California, puts the importance of social class in the most forthright and harshest terms when she writes, "Literacy itself can be understood only in its social and political context, and that context, once the mythology has been stripped away, can be seen as one of entrenched class structure in which those who have power have a vested interest in keeping it" (p. vii). Though schools also speak to "a very real need on the part of all socio-economic classes to learn about and transform the nature of their existence" (Giroux, 1981, p. 184), it is certainly in the interests of students, parents, and teachers at Pepperdine (and I include myself here) to acquire and promote advanced literacy as a source of cultural, economic, and political power.

At least 30 years of research has closely examined the effects of class structure on literacy practices, from Freire's *Pedagogy of the Oppressed* (1970/1982), Sennett and Cobb's *The Hidden Injuries of Class* (1972), and Bowles and Gintis's *Schooling in Capitalist America* (1976) to extensive work in the 1980s and early 1990s by, to name just a few examples, Giroux (1981), Heath (1983), Shor (1987), Berlin (1992, 1996), and Villanueva (1993), as well as many others. More current works, like Sternglass's *Time to Know Them* (1997), Tom Fox's *Defending Access: A Critique of Standards in Higher Education* (1999), Gleason's "Evaluating Writing Programs in Real Time: The Politics of Remediation" (2000), and review articles by Adler-Kassner (2000) and Tinberg (2001), demonstrate how heavily cultural and social class differences influence which students are labeled as "prepared" or "underprepared" for college and what, usually very different, kinds of resources are available for their education.

To describe the social-class landscape of education in our own city, Los Angeles, Mike Rose's *Lives on the Boundary* (1990) is especially instructive. Rose illustrates how class and cultural differences and unequal access to educational resources can mark students as marginal, what Rose calls an "educational underclass." Rose grew up in South Central Los Angeles and struggled to complete college at Loyola Marymount University, another "religious" school situated over the hill and down the freeway from Pepperdine. Rose managed to continue his education at the University of California, Los Angeles, and now teaches there, UCLA, the big school in Westwood, with the highest status in the local, postsecondary scene. Rose chronicles how poverty can place a student outside the boundaries of educational success, how it feels to try to cross boundaries, and the resources needed to make the journey.

If our study students are representative at all, they are the students on the "inside" of that boundary, though some come from families that have only recently and only narrowly crossed from the "margins" to the "mainstream" of class and culture. Like the adults and children described in Barbara Ehrenreich's *Fear of Falling: The Inner Life of the Middle Class* (1989), these students want to keep the advantages their families have accrued and, if possible, improve their status. The literacy practices analyzed in this volume, then, are not simply a generic set of skills, practices indicative of the way advanced literacy in college must be or ought to be, but the specific practices of a specific group of students in a particular time and place.

Four of these specific students—Sarah, Carolyn, Kristen, and Andrea—were introduced in chapter 1. Here, before I go on to analyze their literacy in more detail, I want to briefly introduce our other study students and some examples of key pieces of writing they selected, during their senior year, for their digital portfolios. These profiles and portfolios offer a further introduction to both the similarity and diversity of our students' experiences.

Humanities Majors

Like Sarah, Elizabeth and Terri majored in the humanities. Sarah was a star intellectual in English, and her senior honors thesis, "A Study in Autobiography: Maxine Hong Kingston and the Literary Chameleon," was published by the humanities/teacher-education

division. Unlike Sarah, Elizabeth, who sometimes scraped by with
D's and C's, could not mention a single course or project that truly
engaged her. When pressed, she thought a long time, then considered that she somewhat enjoyed modern British and Irish literature
because it reminded her of the time she spent in London during her
sophomore year. Terri included in her portfolio a test in Religion
301 during the fall of her sophomore year. It was her first "A" in
college. After some writing in her first year about her experience as
an African American woman in Los Angeles, she decided to avoid
topics directly related to her personal experience. She struggled to
modify what she identified as her own voice to write acceptably in
her history major and earned an 88 on her senior thesis, "Shut-door
Theory, Millerites, and Denominationalism: 1845–1846."

Communication Majors

Vanessa was a talented and experienced student writer. For her
digital portfolio, she selected a detailed history of her extended
Mexican-German family, reflections on her experiences as a tutor at
a local juvenile detention facility, and a twenty-page report/analysis
of artist Gustav Klimt. She also included three pieces of her work as
a journalism major: an award-winning newsletter written with two
other students, an article from the college newspaper about Pepperdine's ill-fated choice of special prosecutor Kenneth Starr as dean of
the Law School, and, another article, an in-depth investigative report about drug use on campus.

Natalie, Leslie, Deborah, and Carolyn, who were also communication majors, all had semiprofessional news stories, ad campaigns, and public relations projects to include in their portfolios.
Natalie, the first in her family to graduate from college, financed
her education in part by a $6000 beauty pageant scholarship and
$20,000 in student loans. Although she had an internship with the
Nickelodeon children's network, she also hoped to pursue a career
in entertainment by trying out as a cheerleader for the L.A. Lakers.

Science Majors

Kristen, Randall, and Susanna sat together at a portfolio project
meeting in fall 1997. Their compatriot George was off studying

sports medicine in Australia for the semester. When we talked about writing, these science majors wanted to make sure that they would not be assessed by "English" standards. On a questionnaire filled out at that meeting, Kristen wrote, "I have a difficult time being creative in my writing. I'm so used to being a straightforward writer that I'm rusty on my creativity." Randall responded, "Writing subjectively is very difficult for science majors because we are forced and trained throughout to write objectively and with extreme detail." However, in the winter 1998 semester, Randall selected for his portfolio "Density Control and Distribution of the Great White Shark, *Carcharodon carcharias* Along the North American West Coast" and said this is "where I made a turnaround." He added, "Well, this is the first paper where I took the science data, talked about what was said, what they found, and then what *I* thought, what I thought was either correct or incorrect about their findings."

Social Science Majors

Andrea came to Pepperdine because it offered her the best financial aid package. She was the only political science major in our study. Stephen, Georgia, and Paul were majoring in psychology. Stephen, who was minoring in religion, was difficult to contact as a research subject. Most of his nonclass hours were spent on campus ministry and other extracurricular activities. Georgia's portfolio traced her goal of working with children. It included papers on children's risk factors for depression and on self-esteem and a children's book she had written that also illustrated her interest in art. Paul selected for his portfolio philosophical essays from his Great Books seminars, a response paper on religion in Japan from an Asian studies course, and lab and research reports from his psychology major. He said he could have had a higher GPA but "I guess there are times when I just think there's more important things than doing the work. I've got like a 3.2 now, so it's a decent GPA, and I've had some good social interaction." Although his father was a lawyer and his mother with an M.S. in business ran a family-owned hardware store, Paul worked all summers and every semester, beginning in his sophomore year, including almost 40 hours a week as a manager at Blockbuster Video during fall 1997.

Business Majors

Allison, Jeanette, Julia, and Bhakti, as business majors, selected papers mostly from their general education classes for their final portfolios. When asked about writing in her specialization, business administration, Julia said, "Most of it's just tests and exams. . . . Or, if we do do projects, like, actually we did a big marketing project . . . they keep them, so. . . . well, we turn them in at the end of the semester and then I don't know what happens to them." Allison, in accounting, included one auditing research project in her portfolio, explaining how she conducted a sample audit and drew conclusions and reported succinctly, using numbers and short bullet points of one or two sentences. Allison was the first in her family to graduate from college. Her father was retired from a twenty-year career in the navy and fixed computers. Two months before graduation, Allison already had a job with a major accounting firm in Los Angeles and had received from them a new laptop computer as a perk for signing on at a salary she said was $10,000 more than she had expected to make.

These are the students who agreed to participate in the Digital Portfolio Assessment Project and stayed with us for four years providing data about their college experience. This data was both rich and messy including piles of folders, student self-assessments both on paper and in computer files, and boxes of audio and video tapes.

A Qualitative Methodology for Studying Development

We first seriously examined this data during the summer of 1995 when one instructional librarian and eight faculty members from mathematics, English, communication, biology, and psychology gathered to analyze the portfolios, assessments, audio tapes, and videotapes collected during our study students' first year. Although the Digital Portfolio Assessment Project (DPAP), which provided the data for this study, had from the beginning used qualitative research methods and strategies developed from the contemporary assessment movement, especially as promoted by professional organizations such as the American Association of Higher Education

(AAHE), methodology was a subject of discussion among faculty members from very different research traditions. A literature review essay, "Qualitative Research Methods in Higher Education," (Crowson, 1994) from the comprehensive *Handbook of Qualitative Research* (Denzin & Lincoln, 1994), provided grounding for these discussions. While Crowson acknowledges that there is no single definition of what constitutes qualitative research and that terms such as *ethnographic* or *naturalistic* are contested, he concludes:

> At best, it can be said that to work "in the style" of the qualitative research is to consistently employ such practices of data collection as participant observation, the discovery and use of unobtrusive measures, informal interviewing, life history construction, content analysis, and videotaping—and to seek from one's data *understanding* of the phenomena observed rather than some generalizable knowledge or explanation, prediction, and control. (p. 169)

Crowson's loose definition fit my own sense of how best to research a complex system such as a college general education program and the development of students within such a system. My previous experience as a teacher and department chair at an urban high school, as director of a National Writing Project site, and as an instructor at two independent universities and a professor at a third, Pepperdine, and my work, at different times, as a writing center director and a writing program administrator helped me to observe Pepperdine's programs both as an outsider familiar with quite different settings and as a participant within our general education program. My dissertation had been a qualitative study of an adult literacy project, and I had had previous training in anthropology as an undergraduate and in sociolinguistic research as a graduate student. Crowson's review summarized both the advantages and problems of qualitative research.

My colleagues from different research traditions and I struggled especially to find ways to make sure our qualitative study findings were as trustworthy and creditable as possible. That first summer, we focused not specifically on student writing but primarily on critical thinking and ethical development. The methods we practiced were those I continued and refined in my own research on writing and that have been employed in subsequent DPAP projects. Initially, we read through or listened to data provided by different students, then listed and discussed various perspectives that emerged both from students themselves and our own analysis of their written and spoken words. Based on the data, we wrote thick descriptive profiles of individual students and compared these. As we began to make hypotheses about our findings, we looked for examples that either confirmed or negated our conclusions. Our mathematician, Don Thompson, drawing on rubrics we had developed, devised radar dot graphs on which we could visually plot examples and levels of the critical thinking we observed in the student data. Examples of these graphs, again, are available on the assessment program web site along with more detailed accounts of DPAP history, methodology, and general findings.

As part of a growing interest on our campus in writing across the curriculum and as a result of my own research, a second cross-disciplinary group of nine faculty members reviewed portfolios and other data after our study students' sophomore year. This group also wrote thick description profiles and examined the amount and types of writing students had engaged in during their first two years. Faculty in this second DPAP seminar also analyzed how particular courses seemed to challenge or not challenge students and how students responded to those challenges. Findings from both summer assessment seminars were reviewed in faculty workshops and continue to influence general education reform on our campus.

Although in retrospect I can calmly recount the progress of this research project, in practice, data and findings began to overflow as students reached their junior and senior years. Henry Gambill, our current director of assessment at Seaver College, started work as a research assistant for the project and brought a fresh insider perspective, since he had been a student at Pepperdine and now also taught a first-year writing course and served as a mentor-tutor in our writing center. Don Thompson offered a wider perspective as he became academic dean of Seaver College and continued to work with the project, focusing especially on developing technology to store and effectively present student data. As subsequent summer faculty development seminars focused on other important areas of learning, I continued my own analysis of students' development as writers, formulating working hypotheses and cross-checking these with the data, with study participants, and with colleagues. Because our study continued over several years, I had many opportunities to refine the questions I asked and the conclusions I drew. As I began to know the study students better, I got their responses to my initial hypotheses. I presented parts of this study both on my own campus and elsewhere to different groups of faculty, some in composition, some across the disciplines, who asked provocative questions. I shared findings with students not in the study, particularly our writing center tutors and upper-division students in my course for prospective teachers, asking if my conclusions fit their experiences as writers at Pepperdine. Henry Gambill, Don Thompson, and my colleagues in composition and rhetoric offered many useful insights and helpful critiques.

Slowly the map of student development began to take shape. A central goal of qualitative research is to create an understanding of complex, hard-to-measure human behavior as seen from the observed actor's perspective (Crowson, 1994). At the same time, I, as the observer, must acknowledge my own values, my own role in the environment under investigation, and the previous theories and research that inform my analysis. In tracing the development of participants in my study, I trace my own development as well. In the chapters that follow, I offer both my students' voices and my own. Students' quotes are directly transcribed from taped interviews. When I am drawing from students' written work or self-assessments, I indicate this in the text. Self-assessment forms and interview questions used in the study are included in Appendix A.

Since our initial project, two additional cohorts of students have been studied, in two different projects, as part of ongoing assessments of multicultural awareness and of the impact of service learning. The director of assessment, Henry Gambill, has written two documents, available on the web site described in Appendix A, that further review the history and methods of the Digital Portfolio Assessment Project. Additional documents focus on specific methods and findings of the projects, and there are links to other useful assessment resources.

3 / Riding the Literacy Roller Coaster in General Education and First-Year Composition

> Here the emphasis is not on the traditional psychological pro-
> cesses of perception, motivation, thinking, and learning, but on
> their *content—what* is perceived, desired, feared, thought about,
> or acquired as knowledge, and how the nature of this psycho-
> logical material changes as a function of a person's exposure to
> and interaction with the environment.
> —Urie Bronfenbrenner, *The Ecology of Human Development*

Susanna wrote on a self-assessment that college "forces" students to change their writing. When I asked what she meant, she answered that her English I teacher was "really picky" and "I felt like I had to change the way I was writing in order to kind of fit the professor. I mean, I think that is true in English classes. Every professor is different and so you have to change however you're writing for that professor." This is a truth universally acknowledged and asserted by almost every student in our study. Whenever they are writing for grades, students, in order to be successful, must give professors what they want. Later in their college careers, students may come to see some of the demands of their professors not as idiosyncratic requirements but as conventions of particular academic and professional genres and believe that adapting to these conventions is necessary for becoming a journalist, a scientist, or a psychologist. But as a first step, they must abandon their "normal" ways of writing to adjust to the demands of a new environment and new roles.

Every student in our study produced work in their junior and senior years that indicated new ways of writing that were not evident in their first year. When I discussed portfolios with students and examined major papers and projects from their senior year, I asked them if they could have completed these same projects when they began their college careers. Each student said no. To begin with, most reported that as first-year students sheer length, even five typed pages, intimidated them. Terri's senior history thesis on the Millerite religious movement in the 1840s was only 12 typed pages long, but it was packed with information. Terri explained how she gradually learned to break longer papers into subsections and work on one part at a time. More than mere length, however, students said that as first-year students, they simply did not have the knowledge and concepts to write more complexly and in-depth about specialized topics. Student writing over four years gets "better" according to Scardamalia's (1981) definition of cognitive development, which is "construed as taking progressively more variables into account during a single act of judgement" (p. 82). To complete the complex literacy tasks of their academic disciplines, the variables students must consider include: following appropriate genre and discourse conventions, locating and interpreting relevant sources, applying concepts from the discipline, developing evidence acceptable in the discipline, and organizing all of this information in a single coherent text. All of the students became more adept at juggling these variables; all were successful in earning "B's" and sometimes "A's" on at least some papers and projects in their major fields. However, in balancing all the demands of new ways of thinking and writing in addition to the complexity of their personal lives as maturing, young adults, students rarely were able to produce perfect work.

As they reflected on their own development, students themselves often pointed out that they could not say their writing had gotten "better" because it was difficult to compare senior science or marketing projects to papers written in first-year composition and because they still struggled with new assignments. They could, however, explain how their writing was different—more complex in content and more appropriate to the role of a scientist or business manager. It may seem obvious that, of course, any group of students over a four-year period will come to know more and be able to do more. But this development is not always obvious to professors in individual courses. When professors assign only one paper in a course, they often see what the student cannot yet do, especially when compared to others in the class, and miss this larger picture of individual development. Nonetheless, one might ask if the development we see is simply the result of maturation and "seat time" spent in classes or if there is what my university likes to call true, "value added," growth promoted by the efforts of the institution, professors, and students themselves.

In this chapter, I examine how students' experiences in their first two years of college shape their development as writers. I look closely at some of the specific writing environments students encounter and demonstrate the sometimes painful process that students undergo as they attempt to meet the varying demands of different professors. Writing across the curriculum is a roller coaster with much writing in some semesters and little in others. In their introductory classes in general education, students especially value projects that mark points of transition, milestones in their learning in which they are able to make connections between their writing and their own developing interests and experiences. Some of the best of these literacy projects are supported by "hands-on" learning outside the classroom. Students have few opportunities to write in-depth or develop a particular type of writing over time. First-year writing provides intensive practice and a few basic insights about college literacy tasks that students often can express but may find difficult to apply. A four-semester sequence of Great Books courses offers one opportunity for sustained growth, though, again, the lessons learned do not necessarily carry over to writing in other courses or disciplines.

The experiences of the study students in their first two years of college demonstrate that composition specialists might well follow a dictum of the ecology movement, "think globally, act locally." In the big picture of writing in college, first-year composition is only a small part of a much larger environment. Although it is difficult to make major changes in this global environment, we can most usefully focus on the local, teachable moments of transition, Vygotsky's zones of proximal development, that students already experience and the additional kinds of support that would promote their learning at those moments.

Auditing Writing in Years One and Two

Students' first encounters with "college writing" come in their general education courses, which offer more homogenized versions of the academic discourses they will revisit in their major areas of study. Pepperdine University, a notably conservative institution, has maintained a fairly traditional general-education core curriculum. Students must complete required courses in a variety of disciplines, including English, speech, religion, Western heritage (humanities), non-Western heritage, American heritage, behavioral science, laboratory science, foreign language, mathematics, and a freshman seminar. Students may choose a four-course Great Books sequence that satisfies both the English and freshman seminar requirements and also substitutes for one required course in American heritage and one required course in religion. Pepperdine also offers a well-established program of international studies. Students can use scholarship monies and work-study to pay for these programs, and almost half of our students spend at least a semester studying abroad.

A review we conducted in 1995, when our research students had completed only their first year, revealed considerable variation in the amount and types of writing students did, even when they were enrolled in the same general education courses. For example, even though course guidelines and professors' syllabi indicate minimum requirements for edited, final drafts and an emphasis on academic writing in both English I and freshman seminar, student portfolios told a different story. Some teachers in different sections of these courses required less writing and emphasized more informal, personal responses from students. Students were not wrong in believing that professors' expectations varied widely both within and across disciplines.

While professors across the curriculum may blame students for not knowing already "how to write" or for not quickly becoming better writers, in fact, the number of opportunities, outside of composition courses, that students have to practice writing in response to complex literacy tasks is very inconsistent from semester to semester. Students' writing abilities do not develop in a neat, linear progression from assignments in general education courses, including first-year composition, on to major projects in upper-division classes. Paradoxically, students' rhetorical sophistication may grow because they often receive no consistent instruction in writing and must become adept at figuring out for themselves the expectations of their various academic audiences.

When they entered college, many of our study students, coming from economically advantaged or selective private and public schools, said they thought they were good writers in high school, that they actually liked to write, and several pointed to outstanding high school teachers who had helped them become better writers. In fact, in a survey of the 1994 entering class, 66% rated themselves as above-average writers. While, again, no one student can be representative of a whole group, Carolyn, the public relations major profiled in chapter 1, is a good example of a student with considerable experience in writing in high school, and her portfolio demonstrates the varying literacy tasks, topics, and quantity of writing she encountered during her first years of college.

In her first semester at Pepperdine, Carolyn included in her comprehensive portfolio, collected for our project, 79 pages of out-of-class writing in Biology 110, Speech 180, English 101, and a freshman seminar focused on intercultural communication. The topics she wrote about included: sickle-cell anemia, France, culture shock, a cruise vacation, speech codes on college campuses, President Clinton's speech on Haiti, Ozzy Osbourne, gangs, the stigma of AIDS, and television shows that depict Southern California. Most of these papers required that she summarize or report on some information and offer her own response, analysis, or argument drawing on concepts from the class, the textbook, or personal experience.

In this early work, Carolyn was able to carve out an issue and begin to explore it, even begin to develop an argument, though, in general, she lacked the sophistication both rhetorically and in terms of content to deal with much complexity. For example, in October of her first semester, Carolyn tackled the issue of speech codes on college campuses in a three-and-a-half-page essay. She began by asking several rhetorical questions:

> Political correctness, a figment of the media's hypersensitive imagination or is it truly an issue that should be ranked highly on our "things to take care of" agenda? Many major and minor universities across the nation, believe that political correctness is a problem that needs to be dealt with. Should we, the American public, calmly stand by while people of authority take away our Constitutional right to speak our mind? Our predecessors left their homelands to come to America for their freedom to speak. Are we going to give our rights up without a fight?

Carolyn immediately established a "we," those whose "predecessors left their homelands to come to America for their freedom to speak" as opposed to a "they" identified in a later paragraph as those "minorities, homosexuals, and other groups labeled oppressed" whom speech codes are supposed to protect. She appealed to the shared context of the university where, she argued, students ought to be able to speak freely and listen without censorship. In making her argument, Carolyn drew on articles from *The New York Times, U.S. News and World Report, Newsweek, Dissent,* and *The Quill* as well as a group of articles reprinted in her textbook, *Signs of Life in the USA: Readings on Popular Culture for Writers* (Maasika & Solomon, 1994). This content supplied many examples and arguments that Carolyn measured against the theoretical concept of "freedom of speech."

Carolyn viewed this essay as a successful learning experience, which "helped me to take a stance on a topic that is very popular today." Carolyn did effectively take a stand and develop her argument.

Her view was limited, however, by an oversimplified opposition between "the oppressed" as "others" and the "American public" college student audience, which she assumed (at least for the purposes of this essay) shared her own cultural, sexual, and class values. While she recognized some conflicts in her argument and briefly struggled to separate "fighting words," "harassment," and "free speech," she quickly moved back to her initial position and stuck to her thesis defending an abstract notion of "free speech," avoiding the ambiguities of how speech actually plays out in social relationships. Her teacher, however, acknowledged what Carolyn did well in this essay and gave her 88 out of 100 on the paper. Carolyn's essay was successful because it fulfilled both her own and the teacher's expectations near the beginning of her first year.

Carolyn might be faulted for not thinking more critically in this essay, and critical thinking is supposedly an important goal of general education classes. But Carolyn scarcely had time to think in-depth about the myriad of topics she wrote about in her first semester, from speech codes and gangs to sickle-cell anemia and AIDS. Especially in "skills" classes like English composition and speech, students must write and speak without much opportunity to build the content knowledge that is required to write truly informed critical analysis. Professors who accuse students of being unable to "think critically" often overlook the crucial role of this content knowledge that students will continue to acquire in their more specialized areas of study.

As Carolyn moved into the second semester of her first year, the amount of writing she produced fell dramatically to only 21 pages written outside of class. In English 102, she wrote several analyses of literary works, a genre familiar from high school, and she composed a brief report in Sociology 200. Her Mass Communication 200 course required multiple choice and short-answer tests, and she wrote short compositions in French for French 251. Some general education courses, like Sociology 200, and introductory courses in the majors, like Mass Communication 200, focus on giving students a broad base of content knowledge but do not include much writing. These courses may be taught in large lecture formats making assigning, supervising, and grading writing more difficult. With lots of content but little emphasis on how to read, write, or research in the discipline, these survey courses are the opposite of the skills courses. Presumably, at least in the individual academic majors, writing skills will reappear later when students can apply the knowledge base they have acquired.

Interestingly, Carolyn wrote more during the fall of her sophomore year, which she spent in our international program in London. There, classes tended to be smaller, and most of her courses were taught by British teachers who, like other faculty in our European programs, seemed less inclined to multiple choice tests. Essay tests were the norm. Each course—art history, management, religion, and history of England—fell into the pattern of one, two, or three essay tests and one final paper or project. Carolyn brought home 81 pages of writing, 32 pages written outside of class.

Back in Malibu for the winter semester, Carolyn's portfolio was again slender, only 22 pages, mostly written as in-class essays for Humanities 113. Communication 205 focused on many short grammar and style exercises. Economics 200 and Religion 102 required only objective tests and very short or optional papers.

Finally, in the fall of her junior year, Carolyn's writing turned more toward her major field and a career orientation in public relations. Carolyn's portfolio indicated three project reports and three in-class essays for Public Relations 355, and 33 short exercises and assignments in all mass media genres for Mass Communication 280. In her other classes, Business Administration 320, Personal Finance, required three objective tests and a personal financial plan, Religion 301 included three in-class essay tests, and even Physical Education 124, Beginning Ballet, required two objective tests. Again, the total of finished writing, both in and out of class, was close to 80 pages.

Faculty reviewing portfolios in workshops during the summers of 1995 and 1996 were concerned by the gaps in both the quantity and quality of writing expected from students across different courses. In general, students go from extensive writing in

English and speech courses to more varied experiences in freshman seminars and other general education or beginning major courses, with some courses requiring relatively complex literacy tasks, others asking for more informal, personal responses, and still others assessing students' mastery of course content through problem sets or objective tests. In our portfolio workshops, we rejected the proposition that more writing is automatically better and accepted the premise that courses might legitimately vary in their emphasis on different ways of knowing. Nonetheless, we suspect that the variations in courses that students experience are more by accident than by design. To the extent that students do not demonstrate the knowledge and critical literacy we believe they should have, we need to ask where in the curriculum they will be asked to take on challenging new roles as writers and develop more complex skills.

Writing That Works in General Education

General education by definition introduces students to college-level work in many disciplines outside their academic majors. As Carolyn's experience illustrates, students must learn to write differently but have few opportunities to develop one particular type of writing over any extended period of time. Nonetheless, students' literacy development does continue. When we asked our study students as seniors to review their portfolios and from each year select work that was the most significant or representative of their learning, students rarely had difficulty deciding which work to choose. Their choices from general education courses reflected their experience of a curriculum oriented to both the liberal arts tradition and the production of knowledgeable workers. The writing/literacy tasks that students selected as significant fell into the following different categories:

- major projects that helped students learn new skills
- challenging exams showing the students' integration of knowledge

- academic writing related to personal experience
- writing representing new knowledge and "hands-on" experiences

This writing in general education courses, though sometimes assessed by students as not their "best work," was an important way of learning because it caused students to make connections between their growing skills, knowledge, and personal interests.

Kristen, the sports medicine major profiled in chapter 1, selected her freshman seminar research paper on scoliosis as significant because she said it represented a milestone, her first research paper in college. For Natalie, who majored in public relations, her rhetorical analysis in her speech class of Clinton's 1995 State of the Union address marked a similar milestone in learning to research and write a critical analysis longer and more complex than anything she had written in high school. Several students chose for their final portfolios exams from humanities courses and from religion and culture courses because they also represented difficult tasks they had mastered successfully. Kristen, who spent much time learning to write like a scientist, added to her portfolio her in-class humanities essay on *Othello,* which demonstrated her understanding of a challenging literary work. Deborah, who was frustrated by the conflicting demands of some of her teachers, was proud of her final exam in a religion and culture course in which she was able to "put together everything you learned in the class."

Writing about personal experiences in courses outside of speech or English composition was least represented in students' final digital portfolios. Yet this partly depends on how "personal writing" is defined. Though students did, in their first two years, write about experiences as private as parents' divorces or the deaths of friends or relatives and included these papers in their comprehensive portfolios, they rarely chose these for their final digital portfolios, perhaps because the digital portfolios are a more public forum and also because this kind of narrative or expressive writing, reviewed after a few years in college, seemed less of a milestone in their development. Allison, whose comprehensive portfolio consisted mostly of problem sets from accounting, was an exception in selecting as significant work her speech about the murder of a friend and a eulogy for her grandfather. Other students, like Vanessa writing about her extended Mexican-German family and Bhakti recounting the history of her family's immigration from Pakistan, especially valued work that expressed their personal identities, their sense of who they are, especially in contrast to the more homogeneous student body at Pepperdine. Vanessa's family history was the result of a research project, and Bhakti's autobiography had gone through several drafts. These papers also represented milestones for these students because they were relatively complex analyses, going beyond expressive writing to present the writer's experience convincingly to an unfamiliar audience.

Ultimately, however, all of the writing in students' portfolios is personal because it represents the students' personal experiences with the curriculum. Students perhaps recognize this more clearly than professors. As students reviewed with me their work in general education courses, I was interested in their development as writers. But they could look through their written texts to see themselves making connections between old and new knowledge. Students teach us that student learning is not identical to the written text, a principle that professors are apt to forget. Professors tend to evaluate student papers as text and as representative of what students know or what they have learned in a course and representative of their ability as writers. In order to justify grades, teachers assess what appears on the page, though, of course, like all readers, they also read into the text what they expect to find there. Yet, students in our study repeatedly discussed papers that in the student's own assessment were not great writing but did represent significant learning. It may be comforting for professors to know that even mediocre papers can represent good learning. Leslie, for example, aiming toward a career in marketing, pointed out that her paper analyzing the political condition of the state of California is not "the exact pinnacle" of her writing; however, it demonstrated an important change in her thinking. Before the course, she was not really interested in politics, now she was. Paul explained that his response paper on religion in Japan was not outstanding writing but illustrated his growing interest in Asian culture, an interest partly inherited from his parents, who lived for a time in Taiwan. Paul followed up on this interest by taking an additional art history course on non-Western art.

We will see that in their major fields students continue to look for connections between their own interests and academic learning, finding their own ways through the curriculum. Themes emerge as one reviews their portfolios. Paul from an early speech about his parents' divorce to a major paper describing his theoretical approach to psychotherapy showed a philosophical turn of mind and a strong interest in human relationships. Andrea, majoring in political science, took every course she could related to Africa and African American studies and wrote repeatedly about civil rights issues. Carolyn, negotiating the disparate writing tasks in general education courses, had a practical approach, always interested in how to do things better and more efficiently. For projects in communication, she drew on the extensive writing and speaking she did outside of class for her sorority. These lines of personal development are rarely visible in a single text in a single class.

Writing that brings together academic learning and "hands-on" experience seemed to rate especially highly with students. Nine students in our study independently selected the same type of art history paper as significant work to be included in their digital portfolios. This was the only assignment to appear repeatedly across the group, regardless of major. These papers tended to be relatively long (20 pages), illustrated with photocopied pictures or postcards of artwork, and, in most cases, reported on the work of a single artist chosen by the student—Botticelli, Pissarro, Renoir, and Klimt, among others. These reports of the artist's life and analyses of particular paintings seemed fairly straightforward; at first glance, they struck me as work that could easily be plagiarized, downloaded from the Internet. Significantly, however, seven of these reports were written while students were studying in Europe in either London or Florence, and the other two papers involved visits to local museums in Los Angeles.

Why was this one assignment so significant for students? To begin with, very simply, it looked good in a digital portfolio on a web page. It was one of the few examples of student work in general education classes that was not just straight text, that was interesting visually. Secondly, more importantly, it represented again the value that students placed on work that was challenging and that promoted new learning. In London, this art history paper was called a "dissertation," and the professor required a minimum of 20 pages. Students said this sounded "scary," so they had a solid sense of accomplishment when they completed the assignment successfully. Although the writing in these reports was not always outstanding, again, the texts alone cannot be taken as the only evidence of learning. Students who were not much interested in art or did not know much about it discovered a new interest, a new pleasure. Others had a chance to explore in-depth an artist significant to them.

However, most importantly, students said this assignment represented a "hands-on" experience. In one sense, this experience was the very large, life-changing process of living abroad for a semester or a school year. The art history paper illustrated again that texts represent student learning; they are not identical to it. Every student felt they became more mature and had a greater appreciation of other cultures after their international experience. They wanted something in their final portfolio to represent this developmental milestone, and the art history paper captured a small part of this.

On the other hand, it is not possible to send every college student abroad to experience firsthand all of world history and culture. But students pointed out that the art history paper was also "hands-on" because they went to see real pictures in real museums. Terri, who had struggled to earn "C's" in first-year composition, traveled to several art galleries in London and to Cambridge to seek out work by Pissarro. However, Jeanette and Paul visited museums closer to home in Los Angeles. Students suggested that most classes could be enriched by such excursions into the "real" world or by speakers from the "outside." Terri explained how a speaker from the board that rates movies in England made more concrete for her political science class the issues involved in censorship. Terri worked at the Skirball Cultural Center in Los Angeles and suggested that history and political science students would be interested in attending the Skirball's series of lectures by former U.S. secretaries of state. Other students in our study rated highly the speakers from different religious groups in religion and culture courses and the service-learning projects they carried out at local churches. Such real world experiences may be time-consuming for professors to arrange and for students to complete and so initially meet with resistance. But they are more than just "fun" projects. Especially in general education, students do not necessarily aspire to join the communities to which their professors belong. The knowledge and literacy practices of these communities are represented in the classroom by one, necessarily idiosyncratic professor. "Hands-on" experiences and speakers open the window a little wider to the uses of art, political science, religion, and other specialized areas of study in the environment beyond the university. Students see "real" people who are not getting course credit going to art museums, taking an interest in politics, engaging in service to others. "Hands-on" experiences bring students into these worlds. In terms of literacy development, these experiences expand students' knowledge base, offer new environments and roles to play, and bring together academic and personal learning.

Students in general education courses are likely to remain novices in the types of writing and complex literacy tasks specific to each discipline. They may not understand the expectations of the professor and may need more fully developed assignments, guidelines for performance, models, specific feedback, and opportunities for improvement. Their writing gets better in that they do learn to write differently, but they do not fulfill the fantasy of mastering one kind of literacy, an idealized version of academic writing, which improves consistently over time. Many faculty members, however, assume that this generic form of writing could or should be mastered in first-year English courses and complain bitterly when students who have already completed their composition requirements "still can't write."

Don't They Learn That in English?

At Pepperdine, as in the majority of postsecondary institutions, the most writing intensive courses of students' first year are English Composition I and II. While Pepperdine's first-year writing program is small, from 30–35 sections a semester, and enjoys the benefits of limited class size and a strong writing center, the composition curriculum itself is not so different from that taught at hundreds of other institutions, large and small, around the country. In the two decades from 1980 to 2000, the program experienced all the mood swings and growing pains of the developing field of composition and rhetoric. Currently, all students at Pepperdine are required to complete a two-semester composition sequence unless they have advanced placement credit or choose to take the four-course Great Books option. Students for whom English is not a first language may also be required to complete a pre-English I class, English 100. Unlike many other institutions, we have no basic writing classes at Pepperdine.

Faculty like Professor X in chapter 1, who are faced with student writing that does not meet their expectations, ask why students who have completed English I and II, usually with good grades, still cannot "write." Don't students learn to write in English? Compositionists have sometimes answered that we do not teach "service courses." That is, the role of first-year composition is not to clean up every conceivable student writing problem before students take their presumably more lofty upper-division courses. Nor is there some simple set of "basics" that could quickly be "reviewed" to forestall errors in writing when students get to the real work in their majors. But, of course, this does not answer the legitimate question of what does go on in composition courses.

What is the role of first-year composition? What might students reasonably expect to learn about writing? As noted in chapter 2, the "experienced curriculum," the day-to-day life that goes on in classrooms, is often different from the curriculum described by institutional programs and teachers' course syllabi. Yet that "official curriculum" does provide a blueprint for actual classes. I want to sketch that institutional curriculum at Pepperdine before I describe the experience of our study students. This composition curriculum at Pepperdine was revised in the early 1990s shortly before our study group students began their course work in 1994 and mirrors the changes that were typical in many composition programs at that time. Earlier, in the 1980s, the catalog course description for English I read:

> Intensive training in analytical reading and effective writing. Focus on basic composition with special emphasis on exposition and argumentation. Some training in general research techniques. Writing requirements: 8–10 essays (minimum 8,000 words). Grades given in this course are A, B, C, NC. Prerequisite: ENG 99 or satisfactory score on the English Placement Examination.

Additional requirements included reading "one book-length work and at least eight complete essay-length works." Two essays could be written in class for a midterm and a final, the other six or seven were to be written "out of class." English II followed the same requirements substituting literary readings for the nonfiction essays in English I. This was a fairly standard institutional curriculum in California based in part on something called the "Berkeley Guidelines," requirements set by the University of California (UC) for composition courses that could transfer for credit among all California postsecondary institutions from community colleges to the UC system. It was also fairly enlightened in terms of then current composition/rhetoric theory and pedagogy. At least as described institutionally, students actually did a lot of writing. In English I, this writing was in genres other than literary analysis, the traditional staple of literature classes, and there was not an undue emphasis on grammar review and drill.

Although unusual for a small program, the English department during this period in the 1980s and early 1990s hired three full-time, tenure-track faculty with Ph.D.'s in composition and rhetoric and a fourth tenured compositionist with a Ph.D. in educational psychology. Nonetheless, as tenured faculty have been drawn into administrative duties and upper-division courses, the majority of composition courses have continued to be taught by a few full-time lecturers and many more part-time, adjunct faculty. Because we have only limited graduate programs in the humanities, that additional source of under-remunerated labor often pressed into service to teach composition, graduate students, is not an option at Pepperdine.

Additional guidelines for composition courses continued to develop throughout the 1980s and early 1990s reflecting general trends in the field. For example, a nine page, in-house document, "Guidelines: English 101. English Composition I," emphasizes the writing process, critical thinking, writing for different purposes, and editing errors as part of the revision process. English 99, a remedial writing course, was eliminated. Pepperdine had become more selective in admissions. Composition faculty argued that placement criteria were often inaccurate and that all students could be mainstreamed in small composition classes (18 students) with the support of a well-staffed writing center. Because English I is graded A, B, C or NC (No Credit), students may repeat the course if necessary without injury to their GPA. As it has turned out, however, mainstreaming all students has been successful. We have had no increase in the number of students repeating English I and no calls to return to the English 99 system.

By the time our study group entered Pepperdine in 1994, new catalog descriptions of composition courses were in place. English I was now described as:

> An intensive writing workshop. The emphasis is on reading and writing critically and developing effective writing processes including strategies for generating and researching ideas, drafting, revision, and editing. Students read extensively about current issues and produce portfolios demonstrating their ability to write for a variety of purposes, focusing particularly on academic writing.

English II, continued to be a somewhat conflicted course, supposedly furthering students' experience with "academic writing" but providing the only space in the general education curriculum for extended study of literature and, therefore, still leaning heavily toward literary analysis.

The calm language of the catalog description smooths over the miniculture wars in our small corner of academia. A 1992 memo reads, "Are radical, feminist, deconstructionist, cultural critics taking over English 102 (English II)? No, but we are making a few changes." Each word in the official catalog description of our composition courses could be deconstructed. A continuing emphasis on "process" means students today write fewer papers, are supposed to spend more time revising each one, and are supposed to get more specific feedback from peers, teacher, and the writing center about how each paper could be different, better. "Current issues" generally refers to controversial social issues—the language that shapes argument about diversity, social justice, ecology, political agendas. It might also mean taking action through service learning. "Academic writing" means students generally are not to be rewarded for unpolished narratives of their own experience or polemics expressing personal opinions. They are expected to mimic the supposed conventions of academia in which one responds to and incorporates into one's own text the work of others, constructs an analysis or argument, makes assertions and explicitly develops them. These complex literacy tasks require students to read challenging texts, locate and interpret relevant sources, apply appropriate knowledge and concepts, and ultimately produce coherent, edited written work.

Composition faculty are expected to embody this institutional curriculum in the assignments they construct, the texts they choose, and in their teaching methods. Faculty in workshops and meetings compare syllabi, assignments, books, methods, student papers, and final course portfolios to maintain a degree of uniformity, but we have never had at Pepperdine a common syllabus or a common exit exam for students. In practice, composition faculty, like most other teachers, are independent practitioners once they close the classroom door.

Conflict and Resistance: Altering "Normal" Ways of Writing

To students, the generalized form of academic writing assigned in composition courses, writing that is not constrained by a particular course content to be learned, seems especially subjective and personal, and professors' judgments about what counts as good writing also seem more subjective than in other more fact-oriented courses. Students must change the "normal" ways of writing they learned in high school to meet the expectations of their individual teachers. Brooke and Hendricks' (1989) study of a first-year composition class at the University of Minnesota describes the frustrations of students trying to write for a composition teacher who, in turn, wanted them to imagine how to write for a variety of "real" audiences outside the composition classroom. The students' struggled to negotiate between the unfamiliar forms of writing that might suit these "real" audiences and the "real" teacher who would grade their work. Brooke, the instructor in the course, commendably wanted to teach his students about the concept of audience but seemed as frustrated as his students when he encountered strong resistance and repeated demands from students to know "what he wanted." Students in a beginning ten-week course understandably found it difficult to construct not just persons outside the class who might serve as audiences but also the kinds of evidence, knowledge, forms, and styles of writing that could persuade those persons. During students' first semester in college, the composition teacher is a "real" audience. If students have mastered a "one-size-fits-all" five-paragraph essay in high school, they certainly need to experiment with ways that their writing could indeed be different. But they are likely to resist changing ways of writing that have worked in the past, and they are right to be wary of claims that the concerns emphasized by their particular composition teacher are representative of the concerns emphasized by other academic readers.

While some students are willing simply to accept or even find beneficial the changes they feel they are forced to make in their writing to suit their first-year composition teacher, for others it is a painful obstacle in their transition to college. Natalie, for example, a communication major, accepted that adjusting her style and cutting out extraneous material for her "picky" English I teacher was merely a matter of writing for the audience, something she said she learned in high school although, she added, most of the other students "didn't get it." Bhakti credited her composition teacher with helping her overcome her fear of writing and giving her permission to write from her own perspective as a Pakistani American, a perspective she continued to apply in her psychology classes. But, Allison, who said she went into accounting because she liked right and wrong answers, was simply willing to play the game of school even though, as she explained, some of the topics in her English I class seemed "random and dumb." For example, she had to write on "Do men and women speak the same language?" Her answer was "yes, of course," but she concluded that would not make a good paper. Instead she had to come up with what she called five pages of "fluff," including quotes picked more or less at random from her textbook. Allison echoed the point, "You have to learn what each teacher wants from you," and added that is especially hard for people who "don't have a problem writing."

Several demands made by professors seemed especially onerous. Though teachers maintain they want substantial development and support for ideas, students may feel they are merely adding what Carolyn calls "padding" and Allison calls "fluff." Jeanette, an accounting major, picked for her digital portfolio a paper on the Getty Museum. She said she liked it even if her teacher didn't. She included pictures in her essay instead of writing to the full page requirement. Jeanette said, "I got slapped for the pictures and not enough writing," but writing more would have been "B.S'ing."

More seriously, students complained about having to change their voice, style, and especially their ideas. Russell Durst (1999) in *Collision Course* follows students through two quarters of first-year composition at the University of Cincinnati and examines two powerful sources of conflict between students and teachers. Students complain

> that they are being force fed "a liberal ideology." . . . They worry that the deck is unfairly stacked against them, that they lack the expertise and eloquence to argue effectively against the intellectuals, academics, and professional writers whose work, whose arguments they must respond to. (p. 128)

In addition, students resist the critical stance required in much academic work. They object to being asked to read "what seem to them as unnecessarily abstruse essays and [to] taking on the difficult task of forming and supporting interpretations of what they are finding out are surprisingly complex issues" (p. 128).

Deborah, one of our brightest students, entering with a 1240 SAT and a 3.8 high school GPA, exemplifies how students might reasonably be resistant to both the political and intellectual views of their teachers and the roles they, as students, are asked to play as cultural critics. We chose Deborah's portfolio as one of several to be reviewed in an assessment workshop after the first year of the project. The reviewers, four professors from the humanities, mathematics, and science departments were struck by the contrast between work in Deborah's freshman seminar and her English I class. The freshman seminar called mainly for personal-response writing, graded with few comments beyond "Good!" or "Excellent!" Deborah loved the class. English I, on the other hand, asked her to read books like Cornell West's *Race Matters*. When she and several other students wrote a collaborative book review arguing that West promotes racist views of Whites, the professor probed their responses with what the portfolio reviewers saw as thoughtful and constructive questioning. The portfolio reviewers felt the class did a model job of challenging Deborah to think and write more critically. Yet Deborah titled her final portfolio for English I "Not Black or White," and she included optical illusion drawings, such as an image that can look like either a vase or two faces in profile. In her preface to the portfolio, she referred to all the readings in the course as "literature" and wrote:

> As you journey through the collection, focus your mind not on whether you agree or disagree with my thoughts, but consider the ideas to be valid and valuable, supported opinions coming from the way I see things. Enjoy yourself and ponder your own ideas about the subjects that are dealt with in the collection. In deciphering literature there are no right answers. Everything depends on the point-of-view you take on. The illustrations are included so you can see there are many different ways to look at something. The answers in literature are *Not Black or White*.

In her year-end self-assessment, Deborah said she did not like this class because her professor was not able to consider her point of view. From Deborah's perspective, the professor was a liberal and she was a conservative; he was biased and did not like her ideas. Though the portfolio reviewers, other professors, saw Deborah's teacher as appropriately asking her to challenge her own basic assumptions, Deborah experienced this as unfair and as being "graded down" for her opinions.

It is easy to dismiss Deborah's assessment as a type of relativism typical of young college students moving developmentally from believing there is one right answer to believing there are no right answers. We wondered if by the end of her senior year, Deborah would come to "appreciate" the emphasis on critical thinking in her English I class. But Deborah did not select any work from English I to include in her final, digital portfolio. She said this writing was not representative of her work at Pepperdine. Although she politely acknowledged that she did well enough in English I and learned something, she maintained it was "frustrating fighting between my own writing techniques and my own issues and the professor's ideas . . . even if I argued something well, I found if he didn't agree with my argument, it would get red all over my paper." Looking back on the class, after three years as a telecommunications major, she said,

"[Now] I know more how to handle an English class. . . . I'd try to maybe find more evidence so he couldn't attack me." The lack of evidence or content to develop their arguments, perhaps, helps explain students' real frustration when arguing against the views of their professors. Students are not wrong in supposing it is more difficult to convince an audience that disagrees with one's position, even when that audience is supposedly "objective." Students like Allison may just go along with what the professor wants to hear; others like Deborah try to construct their own opposing arguments but still must work with those random quotes from a text usually chosen by the professor.

Deborah was not simply averse to accepting criticism. She pointed to one of her telecommunications classes where she said the teacher, a professional with years of telecommunications experience, was very critical and even harsh in tone. Yet, Deborah felt this criticism was not personal but was based on what actually works in television news. She felt that having her student projects "torn apart" was supporting her goal of becoming a professional in telecommunications and that the teacher only wanted the students to be successful in getting jobs. Although standards of what "works" are also subject to opinion, students are more likely to see these as standards existing outside the student's or teacher's subjective experience. Students are more willing to adopt the literacy skills associated with the career roles they wish to play.

This is not to say that professors in first-year composition courses should avoid controversial topics, challenging students' ideas, or invoking the sometimes abstract standards of academic, scholarly writing not intended for the business office, newsroom, or science lab. On the other hand, teachers need to accept that conflict is likely when writing concerns personal issues of race, gender, culture, and politics; when the "factual" content of the course is limited; when the professor's worldview is quite different from the student's; and when the student does not necessarily aspire to join the academic communities to which the professor belongs. Composition teachers need to take seriously students' questions about "what the professor wants" as they continue to challenge students to grow within their "zones of proximal development." In the process, faculty need to negotiate with students as they resist and make often quite reasonable attempts to sort out the roles they are and are not willing to play.

Classroom conflict and resistance are especially painful for those students who see themselves as outside the mainstream campus culture. These students may find it even more difficult to make their case to the "expert" professor. Terri, after struggling throughout her first year to write about her own experience in her own voice, made a conscious choice to avoid personal topics for the rest of her college career. Although she originally wanted to be an English major, after receiving C's in both English I and English II, she decided to switch from the "subjective" discipline of English to history where she felt interpretation was based more on facts. Terri, who graduated from a selective, public "magnet" high school in urban Los Angeles, began college enthusiastically and tackled for her freshman seminar a paper on the "Mass Media's Role in the L.A. Riots." Terri said that as a senior in college, she would never have chosen such a topic. It was too broad and, certainly, as a first-year student, she really didn't know how to research it. But she had lived through the 1992 riots in Los Angeles and, as an African American, had objected to the way the media covered her community. She was excited to find many articles in the library that supported her own criticisms of the media. The professor, however, made no written comments on the content of Terri's paper and corrected the style of sentences like the following, "What was omnisciently left out of the clip shown to the public, but shown to jurors in the trial, was the segment before the beating where King had taken no effect to stun guns," which the teacher rewrote as "stun guns had no effect on King." Terri accepted that the teacher's corrections could have made the paper better but said that, even as a senior, "the way I write is the way I talk" and that she herself would not have known how to write her sentences in any other way. She was still proud of this first-year paper and included it in her digital portfolio.

Terri had more difficulty in her English classes. English I was an example of end-of-the-semester portfolio grading gone wrong. She received no grades and mostly positive comments on her work all semester, so she was shocked by a "C" grade on her final portfolio of papers. But English II taught by an African American professor with a special focus on "The African American Dream" was a greater disappointment. Terri says,

> I took this class because it was African American lit and when I got in there, it wasn't what I thought it was going to be. . . . I related stories in the book to my story. I thought this was good, but he (the professor) thought I didn't do enough about the story. . . . I thought by relating it to my life he would understand I knew about the book as well. . . . The writing was too personal. . . . I can identify . . . I make my experience part of it, but I think I did it too much.

Again, this is not to say the professor was wrong in asking Terri to go beyond her personal experience in her writing, but, Terri said, since then "I've tried to stay away from subjects I'm emotionally involved with." For example, she considered taking an African American film class her senior year but thought "it's just going to bring up issues I don't necessarily want to talk about all the time." Although ultimately successful as a history major, Terri explained that she struggled because she often did not understand what the professors wanted. Like other students, Terri experienced an ongoing conflict between her "normal" ways of writing and the demands of academic discourse, but additionally, she was constrained by those invisible boundaries described by Mike Rose (1989), Victor Villanueva (1993), and others. Terri was very soft-spoken, she worked long hours to earn money throughout her college years, and she did not always attend class regularly. In retrospect, she reflected that she rarely talked to her teachers about her writing or worked in study groups with other students and that she probably should have. She had to find her own way through the curriculum, at considerable personal cost.

What Composition Can/Not Teach

The impact of English I and English II is difficult to assess four years later when students seem barely able to remember their first-year courses. When they can recall first-year classes, students certainly do not see composition as the only influence on their literacy skills but also point to other general education courses, especially a required speech course, which provides a similar workshop setting for developing reading, research, and communication skills. As our study students struggled to meet the demands imposed by different teachers in these courses, they did indicate in their self-assessments that they valued work in which they could see their own growth as writers. This growth generally involved rather homely literacy skills such as using sources effectively, improving style, writing for an audience, and learning to organize and develop a complex analysis instead of, as one student put it, just "dumping out your brain."

Despite a heavy emphasis on critical literacy and social consciousness by many of our composition teachers in their courses, it was particularly difficult to trace the later influence of such courses on students' thinking about social issues. While composition teachers can produce student papers and evaluations that show how students change in their thinking as well as their writing over the course of a semester, by the time students are seniors, these changes in consciousness are subsumed in the much larger experience of having lived four years in a more diverse environment and being initiated into specific academic disciplines. Students' worldviews certainly change over four years but a composition course is just one small point of transition that may or may not reinforce students' previous beliefs or contribute to changing them.

A one or two semester composition course in the students' first year cannot teach students to write as experts in specific disciplines or as expert social critics. Students can, however, write as informed nonspecialists and as adult citizens in a democracy, analyzing issues that affect their lives. Within this context, students in our study valued what they saw as improvements in their written texts and in a better understanding of writing strategies they could use in other settings. For example, when Carolyn reviewed her portfolio as a senior, she pointed to her research paper on a speech by President Clinton about Haiti and an analysis of *The Great Gatsby* as two significant pieces of writing from her first year. Carolyn said that while she didn't exactly "plagiarize" in high school, she learned during her first year of college how to use sources and not just copy them with a few words switched around. In English II, Carolyn said that in order to sound intelligent and take up space, she wrote sentences like the following:

> In researching the biography of F. Scott Fitzgerald, it is very apparent how the three of these areas are affiliated with one another. Fitzgerald was strongly affected by his society and the occurrences in his life; therefore these aspects carried on to his writings.

Although she had usually gotten "A's" on her writing in high school, Carolyn reported that the careful comments and corrections of her first-year composition teacher helped her realize that she still lacked what she called "basics" and that she needed to work on style.

When students pointed out changes in their writing, they most often mentioned learning from rewriting, a process that one student explained as "critiquing, redoing, and editing." Several students described working closely with the teacher and revising. In redoing her papers, Jeanette, an accounting major, said she was able to transform her good high school writing from "acceptable to excellent." Reviewing their portfolios as seniors, students recalled the "basics" they became aware of in composition courses. Most importantly, Julia, a business administration major said she learned that you have to show why something is important; "You can't just dump out your brain." Natalie, studying public relations, said her composition class emphasized writing for an audience and added, "You need to cut out extraneous material." Leslie, who had completed several group projects in her marketing major, reflected, "I learned how to set up the paper with transition sentences and to go into details. . . . it's amazing, when I'm working in groups a lot of people don't really know how to set up their papers like that, so it's really helpful."

These "basics," related to research, style, audience, organization, and analysis, are the kinds of writing strategies that students see as most transferable to future writing tasks and, therefore, most useful to their development as writers. I believe that these writing "skills" should be explicitly addressed as part of the composition curriculum. But, paradoxically, these "basic skills" cannot be taught reductively. For students making the transition from their "normal" ways of writing in high school to more complicated literacy tasks, the challenge is to employ their "basic skills" at greater levels of complexity or, in Scardamalia's terms, "taking progressively more variables into account during a single act of judgement." This development can only take place in rich, sometimes messy, literacy environments that coax, or perhaps force, students to go beyond the kinds of reading, writing, and thinking with which they are already comfortable.

Ideally, composition teachers as experienced practitioners with a specialized knowledge of writing processes work within the student's zone of proximal development, helping the learner, in Vygotsky's (1978) terms, complete tasks that "with assistance today she will be able to do by herself tomorrow" (p. 87). Processes such as brainstorming; freewriting; examining models; planning with lists, outlines, or graphic organizers; writing multiple drafts; making use of peer and teacher response; revising; and editing are tools writers can use to work their way through complex literacy tasks. Do these processes transfer to future writing tasks? In chapter 4, students do mention using some of these strategies, but only in particular instances. Generating ideas and planning take on many different forms as students move into different methods of research and data collection. Students usually do not have time to seek peer review and write multiple drafts unless a course is structured to encourage a more extended writing process for challenging writing tasks. Editing is often last minute and frequently haphazard.

However, to ask if writing processes typically practiced in

composition transfer to other settings is perhaps the wrong question. To begin with, if these tools help the novice writer take on more difficult literacy tasks in the time and space of the first-year composition course, then these strategies have value in this setting even if students do not continue to use them in quite the same ways in the future. Secondly, it seems that students do internalize the concepts behind the specific tools. In their "normal" way of writing, beginning students might easily produce a one-draft essay based primarily on experience or opinion. But they come to understand that more difficult tasks in college require additional strategies for gathering information, planning, organizing, and meeting the expectations of readers. As students' comments in chapter 4 will indicate, writers pick and choose and develop their own most efficient writing processes. Professors across the disciplines help when they design assignments with timelines that discourage last-minute writing, when they share their own "tips of the trade," and when they "remind" students to use strategies they have previously learned. Students may continue to use general rhetorical strategies even though they have discarded a particular tool that helped them develop the strategy. For example, one of my students, Chris, in a recent composition course worked with me for two semesters writing papers that were very fluent in style but never quite convincing in content. For one assignment in my class, students experimented with making rhetorical outlines explaining how each section of their essay was meant to affect a reader. This was an "aha" moment for Chris. The rhetorical outline helped him more fully grasp the idea that writing was not only a vehicle for expressing his own thinking but that he could strategically structure his discourse to persuade readers to take his arguments seriously. Although Chris did not continue to make formal rhetorical outlines, he began to write more effectively, not simply lost in his own stylish prose but actually enjoying his ability to influence me and his peer readers. The rhetorical outline served as a tool to move him to a new level of development.

Beyond "basic" writing strategies and processes, students described learning in their composition courses a type of writing they found more personal, more creative, and, unlike the writing in their academic majors, more suitable for a general audience. Surprisingly, despite the conflicts of the composition classroom, many students in retrospect also described this writing as more "fun." These descriptive terms initially surprised me. Our composition courses supposedly emphasized analytical writing, not personal narrative, and assignments generally asked students to think critically about serious issues, often responding to readings or incorporating research, not simply reporting personal opinion. We had hoped to create the kind of rich literacy environments that would challenge our students and teach a generalized form of academic writing that students could adapt for their work in other courses. But, from the perspective of our study students, this generalized form of academic writing, not tied to a specific discipline, still seemed to be lacking in content and more subjective than work in their majors. Although Andrea did say that English II improved her writing in general, she contrasted English composition with more "factual" writing in her political science major. She said, "Freshman year was more creative writing. . . . You have more leeway when you first get here, in your writing. I mean, the professors, they want you to show your true voice. And then you work around that." She added that she thought she was good in creative writing and that she tried to be descriptive and choose just the right words to get her point across. However, she continued, "In my major you just leave all that out and just want the facts. . . . They want specifics, so I had to pay more attention to specifics instead of trying to fit the whole picture." Vanessa, a journalism major, reported,

> I don't think English I and II did much for analytical . . . it's more self-attained knowledge. . . . you would come up with your own ideas and your own thesis and your own support. You would have to take it from yourself and your knowledge. But for journalism, you have to dig. . . . you have to have outside sources, outside quotes, outside interviews with people. . . . if it were my English paper, it would be my opinion and my theories and my thesis and with

journalism articles it's more like here are all the facts, this is why the story is important right now.

Nonetheless, some students saw value in this writing they perceived as more personal and subjective. Again, several said it was "fun," a reason for writing that is, unfortunately, too rarely honored in academic circles. (Writing has to be painful, doesn't it?) They also explained it is a style of writing they "went back to" in writing for other general education classes or for nonacademic purposes. Andrea said about her English I class, "It was fun. It was like a breather. You get to write what you feel," and "the content of the course [women's studies], yes, I think it was very helpful." She added that when she wrote her personal statement for law school, she wanted to have "that frilly stuff" from English I and appeal to emotion. Randall explained how difficult it was, after two years as a science major, to write a comparison of Donatello's and Michelangelo's sculptures of David during a summer of study in Italy. He said, "It was using my mind in a different way. . . . I was so used to having a set schedule in mind of how a paper is written. . . . I needed to remember back to my freshman year and think how this English class was talking about critiquing and analysis." Allison, majoring in accounting, pointed out that students rely more on their English composition experience when their majors, like hers, do not include much writing. Jeanette, also in accounting, noted that she was able to use her English I skills in her other general education classes because they required a similar format of introduction, thesis, and support. Susanna, also a science major, chose "Elvis and Madonna" from English I, and her paper on love poetry from English II to include in her digital portfolio. Her self-assessment noted that "Elvis and Madonna" was fun but also challenged her to go beyond the writing she did in high school because "college writing forces students to be more creative, to adjust their style, and to pay more attention to detail." The poetry paper represented "like an advancement in literature almost just because I was like, oh, ok, poetry's not so bad. . . . "
Susanna and some of the other students seemed to equate the

more "creative" work in English with "real" writing or writing skills in general. Several of these students initially told me their "writing" had not improved much in college, despite evidence to the contrary in their portfolios, because, as Susanna said, "It's been more this research-type stuff that I've been writing." Susanna added, "So, if you told me to take English II again . . . there might be a slight regression from the end of taking that and right now." Andrea also said her writing had not improved because writing in her political science major was more concrete. She gave an example, "You know, I had to write a brief, which is totally different than, you know, a paper that you would have to do." Both Susanna and Andrea, when they reviewed the more complex assignments they had completed successfully in their majors, were reluctant to identify this as improvement. As Andrea said, "I really can't say how my writing has improved because it's on two different levels from when I first came here." And Susanna agreed, "Yah. I guess I'm just separating the two kinds of writing."

In fact, students' recognition of different levels or different kinds of writing is in itself evidence of their growing rhetorical sophistication. There is no generalized, normal, one-size-fits-all type of writing. English I is most valuable, then, not in teaching one particular genre of writing but in creating situations in which students must consider different forms of writing for different, often complex, purposes and employ the kinds of writing strategies that enable them to complete challenging literacy tasks successfully. In addition to practicing writing, they can begin to think rhetorically about their performance as writers. As Bruner (1996) argues, "Achieving skill and accumulating knowledge are not enough. The learner can be helped to achieve full mastery by reflecting as well upon how she is going about her job and how her approach can be improved" (p. 64). This metacognitive awareness is central to development.

Composition courses, then, have value specifically because they provide a time and place in the curriculum where students can examine and practice new forms of literacy without the added requirement of learning a particular subject matter. At the same time, however, composition courses that seek to develop critical literacy face the dilemma of asking students to analyze complex social issues without the body of information and concepts that underlie critiques from particular perspectives in the social sciences, natural sciences, the humanities, and other disciplines.

Examining writing in students' portfolios suggests that teachers need to find a balance between the "what" and the "how" of critical literacy. Students need information and concepts to think about and to think with but also need to focus explicitly on developing new literacy strategies. At Pepperdine, our current composition courses tend to mimic the complexity of academic literacy by choosing a particular theme as "content" for the course and asking students to engage complexity in their reading, writing, and thinking about these themes. The subtitles of English I and English II courses indicate the interests of teachers and the themes students can choose, such as "America on Film," "Writing for the Earth," "Women's Lives," "Civil Laws and Civil Rights," and "Writing and Citizenship." Linking writing and reading assignments to a single theme gives students a chance to choose topics related to their own interests and to build some knowledge about issues rather than randomly addressing a series of disparate subjects.

However, the most important "content" in the course remains the student's own writing. Composition can explicitly teach reading, research, and writing strategies for addressing complex literacy tasks, strategies that are often tacit in discipline-specific courses. These strategies can be practiced over time in a composition course with continuing feedback from a teacher who is an expert in showing novices how their reading, writing, thinking might be different, better. The required first-year speech course at Pepperdine also provides a similar workshop setting for practicing these new skills.

Of course, in the composition program, we, as teachers, experience our own conflicts and resistance. We have resisted pressure from, no doubt, well-meaning but uninformed faculty who think that what our students really need is a thorough review of grammar. We try to demonstrate, partly through the portfolio assessment project, that the real "basics" students must practice are much more complicated. We have also resisted linking composition to fresh-man seminars or other courses, except when teachers have wanted to collaborate closely with each other and both teachers have the development of critical literacy as a primary goal. We have rejected offers of the "I'll handle the content, and you handle the writing" variety as missing the point that knowing and ways of knowing are intimately connected. We fear separating these in students' percep-tion and practice, especially if the discipline-specific course, often taught by a more senior professor, is perceived as the "real" course and writing is just an "add-on." Nonetheless, one program of linked courses on our campus does offer an alternative approach to literacy that illustrates from another perspective that writing does improve with practice but, again, always in context-bound ways that do not necessarily transfer directly to new setting.

Writing Development in a Great Books Program

Though simply linking courses together with concurrent enroll-ment does not insure collaboration or common goals, one might, of course, imagine a general education sequence that would give stu-dents much more consistent instruction in reading and writing. Such learning communities can focus on intellectual and personal development as well as on a particular content. At Pepperdine, this learning community approach is represented in a Great Books pro-gram that enrolls about fifteen percent of the first-year class. The Great Books Colloquium is a four-course sequence of seminars in which students read, discuss, and write about traditional Western classics from Homer and Plato to Nietzsche and Freud. Students receive credit for English I and II and three additional general edu-cation requirements. The Great Books Colloquium is located in the very heart of the conservative liberal arts tradition, in the past re-served for men of wealthy families who did not need to worry about career skills, but now marketed as cultural capital and an opportu-nity for personal growth to the daughters and sons of the middle and upper class.

While one might disagree, and I do, about what students read, write, and discuss in seminars labeled "The Great Books," as an example of writing development, it is instructive to examine the experience of the six students in our study who selected the Great Books option. The type of writing required in Great Books, with a few exceptions, is a highly text-based, thesis and support essay typical of English literature classes. The four-semester sequence of seminars works in that students definitely get better at writing what students call "Great Books papers." Their writing in this format becomes increasingly more sophisticated and more complex over two years.

The Great Books Colloquium course-sequence illustrates several basic principles about the acquisition of literacy. First, students do best what they do most. Programs committed to developing particular ways of writing will provide guided practice over extended periods of time. Secondly, providing such practice with consistent feedback is generally expensive, requiring an extensive commitment from faculty and students. Such programs would be difficult to replicate on a large scale with underpaid, part-time adjunct teachers or graduate students. And finally, even though students become proficient in a particular type of writing in a well-structured program over several semesters, that type of writing is a specific genre necessarily shaped for a specific purpose and audience. Again, there is no universal form of academic writing. While the "Great Books paper" has value in itself as a way of writing and thinking, it is like all other genres not directly transferable to other writing situations.

Still, all of the students who chose Great Books, except Elizabeth, who felt unprepared and overwhelmed by the amount of reading, identified their participation in the colloquium as a highlight of their college experience, an opportunity to think critically about books and their own ideas. Julia, Paul, and Sarah described themselves as students who very much liked reading and were strong writers in high school. Nonetheless, these students too struggled with the perennial problem of giving professors what they want. Despite the general thesis-support format of the "Great Books paper," each Great Books professor varied somewhat in how much writing was expected and in preferences of topic, organization, and style, and Sarah especially struggled to compromise between her personal style and that of each professor.

Paul, however, pointed out how his writing in the Great Books format became more sophisticated over four semesters. An early paper in the first seminar, Great Books I, was a straightforward comparison and contrast essay that began:

> Characters in Homer's *The Iliad* and characters in Aeschylus' *The Oresteia* both had to deal with divine intervention from the Greek gods. Gods in both books seemed to look out for mortals whom they cared for. In *The Iliad*, gods would often lend a helping hand to a soldier who they felt needed help, or would change the course of battle to their liking. An example of one such instance was when Zeus told Hector to keep close to the wall of Troy during Agamemnon's aristeia, for fear that Hector would be injured. The same holds true in *The Oresteia*, even though the methods the gods used were somewhat different. At one point during *The Eumenides*, Apollo defended Orestes, as he tried to escape The Furies in his (Apollo's) temple. This episode was different from a typical episode in *The Iliad* in that Apollo spoke to Orestes directly and in his true form. In *The Iliad*, gods would often disguise themselves, and trick mortals into doing what they wanted done. In *The Oresteia*, gods simply appeared in their true form to mortals, speaking to them directly.

This basically competent, prosaic paper continued with assertions about similarities and differences supported by examples from the texts. Paul's own assessment as a senior was "it's kind of shallow. It's kind of dry on some themes that were pretty clear in the text and kind of talking about them and, maybe, not a whole lot of analysis, some."

By the final seminar, Great Books IV, Paul said, "You're kind of allowed to put in your own ideas and interpret, maybe pull more obscure themes out of what you read." He chose as an example his essay entitled "Time Flies When You're Having Fun" on Thomas Mann's *Magic Mountain*. Near the end of this essay, after analyzing events and using quotes from the novel to raise questions of "man's" (Paul's usage) significance in the face of infinite time, Paul wrote:

> Luckily for us, Mann does not seem to leave these questions unanswered. At the beginning of chapter seven, Mann discusses time once again. He states that "time is the medium of narration, as it is the medium of life" (Mann, p. 541). It would seem to follow from earlier assumptions of Mann's that the eternity of time holds meaning in that it is the medium in which everything exists. All of those conceptions of distance and finite bodies in the universe hold meaning in that they help create the fabric of life that exists as time progresses. True, when compared to the grand scheme of things, one week on one small planet of the universe is hardly worth mentioning. If all of those weeks across the universe ceased to exist, however, there would be nothing worth mentioning or narrating about in the medium of time.

Paul continued this paragraph with a quote from Mann on narration and several more sentences discussing time and meaning before moving on to a rather abrupt conclusion. Though loosely structured and sometimes vague in style, Paul tackled greater complexity in this essay and was able to analyze in more detail the ambiguities of a challenging literary work. He had greater confidence in asserting his own perspectives on themes in the novel. He said this essay reflected his enjoyment of "thinking about my place in the universe."

Having a four-course sequence focused on one kind of reading and writing certainly improves students' skills with this type of reading and writing. In one way, Paul got almost too good at writing in the Great Books format. Saying he was getting "burned out" by the end of Great Books IV, he explained that he quit reading the books and was able to write acceptable essays anyway by choosing a theme discussed in class and skimming the text for supporting quotes. For students, however, writing was only one element, and not the most important feature, of this course sequence. More importantly, they credited the seminars with challenging them to read difficult material, to discuss, and to think critically.

Did students' learning experiences in these classes carry over to work in their academic majors? For Sarah and Elizabeth, the approach to reading, thinking, and writing in Great Books was very similar to their work as English majors, though as I will explain in discussing writing in the academic disciplines, Elizabeth later learned more specific critical approaches to texts and Sarah, as a philosophy minor, discovered a more rigorous analytical method. Stephen found opportunities in Great Books to write about his concerns about religion. Paul, Julia, and George maintained that although their majors required very different kinds of writing, it was useful to know how to read carefully and interpret what texts said and to know how to state an idea and support it.

Several factors beyond "time on task" contribute to the efficacy of this program in developing a particular way of writing, reading, and thinking. Great Books seminars are taught by full-time faculty, usually highly experienced teachers, who meet in a retreat each year to discuss goals and teaching strategies. Although the program is described as interdisciplinary, the majority of teachers are like-minded professors in the humanities, especially English. Classes are small, limited to 16 students. The students who select the program make a commitment to extensive reading and discussion and, presumably, are people who find their own concerns adequately reflected in work primarily by Western, White, male writers. Although Great Books is open to any student, many faculty advisors in the humanities especially promote it for humanities majors.

This expensive seminar sequence is, in a sense, subsidized by composition and other general education courses taught by adjunct faculty and, in some cases, in large lecture halls. It enjoys the support of the senior faculty who prefer teaching Great Books to teaching first-year composition and of administrators who sell the program to prospective students, parents, and conservative donors. The university has been unwilling to provide equal funding, especially in terms of salary for full-time faculty, in programs like composition and speech which serve larger constituencies.

Some features of the Great Books Colloquium, however, are worth replicating if programs are adequately planned and funded. Sequences of courses might be built around other areas of emphasis —ecology, social justice, the arts, alternative selections of "great books." Such sequences would necessarily involve small groups of students and faculty since self-selection seems an important principle. Learning communities like these could again address the balance between "what" and "how," integrating knowledge from several disciplines and providing more opportunities for "hands-on" learning while maintaining an emphasis on literacy development over a period of time more extended than the typical one semester course.

Teaching the Real Basics

In the quote that begins this chapter, Bronfenbrenner (1979) notes that the emphasis in a cultural/environmental view of development is not on traditional psychological processes but on the content of those processes, "*what* is perceived, desired, feared, thought about, or acquired as knowledge, and how the nature of this psychological material changes as a function of a person's exposure to and interaction with the environment" (p. 9). The *what* of students' writing development includes their perception of the conventions of "college writing," their desire to produce writing that is at least "good enough" for success in their classes, their fear of losing their own beliefs and voices, their growing awareness of different types of writing, and their knowledge of different disciplines that is gradually acquired through their course work and out-of-class experiences.

In general education classes, the gap between students' ideas of "normal" ways of writing and the expectations of professors representing specialized academic disciplines may be especially large.

Faculty may underestimate the complexity of the tasks they assign and have little idea of the kinds of writing students are, or are not, doing in other courses. Literacy tasks are especially difficult for students during their first two years of college because of the variety of new tasks they face and because students lack the basic disciplinary concepts necessary for developing in-depth critical analysis. Faculty may address this difficulty in several ways. Professor X simply continues to assign challenging assignments, provides little support in completing them, and, when students fail, blames the students for not knowing already "how to write." Deborah's freshman seminar teacher, on the other hand, assigns only expressive writing, responds only with supportive comments, and does foster Deborah's personal growth but does not encourage a more critical literacy.

Students in the study, however, demonstrated that they did value challenging tasks when they could apply what they had learned in a course or through "hands-on" experience. They also valued instruction and support in learning "basic skills." Students pointed to courses and projects in which they learned rather homely skills like how to use information resources or the idea that one generally needs to have a point or make some sort of argument in academic writing. Students recalled learning some new ways of organizing writing or improving their style through the patient efforts of a teacher willing to work with them in the process of "critiquing, redoing, and editing." A focus on these general skills need not be reductive. The conflicts engendered as faculty push their conceptions of appropriate ways of writing and critical thinking against students' conceptions of what is "normal" can be a wedge to open discussion of what counts as "information," "a point," "evidence," or "appropriate content and style" in a particular discipline. Conflicts can be addressed directly only if faculty work hard at being clear about what they do and why they do it, if they avoid dismissing students' concerns about "what the professor wants" simply as ignorance or "resistance," and if they accept that such conflicts may be painful and, often, unresolved. For students, grades symbolize the power of the teacher to "force" them to change their writing, and in this area especially, faculty need to be explicit about their criteria, ideally supplying models of what it means in their course to "discuss" an issue or write a "well-organized" argument.

Even with instruction and support, the performance of these novice students varies from task to task in their transition from high school to college. First-year composition creates a space in the curriculum for students to think directly about conventions of writing and provides practice in needed "skills," demonstrating ways to use libraries and technology, ways to construct texts and revise and edit. Theoretically, this knowledge about writing could be developed elsewhere in content-based courses across the curriculum and, in fact, much of what students know about writing must be developed in this way. However, first-year composition has value at the beginning of students' college careers precisely because, in this course, they do not need to "cover" a specific content in addition to examining their own writing and knowledge of writing is more likely to be made explicit, rather than implied as in many courses in other disciplines.

This course, however, does not fulfill the fantasy that student writing can be "fixed" when they begin college, so that no further direct instruction will be necessary. No curriculum innovations in composition courses can alter the reality that student writing develops over time as students encounter a variety of new writing environments and acquire greater knowledge of concepts and content. While every college and university maintains that it values critical thinking, students scarcely have time to think very deeply about the many topics they are asked to consider in general education courses, and their opportunities to practice critical thinking in writing are highly inconsistent from semester to semester. Linking courses together is one way to achieve more coherence but this requires close cooperation between faculty, and even in two or three linked courses, students will not develop expert knowledge. The Great Books Colloquium, over four semesters, demonstrates that time and money spent in a well-thought-out program can help students perfect a particular genre of writing, while they engage in challenging discussions of important ideas, but may preclude the opportunity to study a more diverse curriculum. And, even, if students do become relatively proficient in one form of academic writing, we will see in the next chapter that they still must learn new skills as they study biology, psychology, or other disciplines.

Ongoing assessment across disciplines would be one way of identifying exemplars of what sorts of writing and what indicators of critical thinking might reasonably be expected of first and second-year college students. Such assessments of general education would also note where students have opportunities to develop these writing abilities and consider how the environment of general education might be restructured to eliminate the roller-coaster effect of much writing and research some semesters and little in others.

Throughout their transition from high school to college, the written papers of our study students rarely demonstrated the full depth of their learning. Their writing was often just "good enough" to get the desired "B" or "A" grade before they moved on to the next task. Yet, their growing ability to comment on their own work indicated that they were developing greater metacognitive awareness and, in Bronfenbrenner's (1979) terms, "a more extended differentiated, and valid conception of the ecological environment" (p. 27). The next chapter shows that as they make the transition into the environments of their major areas of study, students continue to struggle with "what the professor wants" but also begin to internalize more complex disciplinary knowledge and conventions.

4 / Supporting Writing Development Across Disciplines

> So back to the innocent but fundamental question: how best to conceive of a subcommunity that specializes in learning among its members? . . . Typically, it models ways of doing or knowing, provides opportunities for emulation, offers running commentary, provides "scaffolding" for novices, and even provides a good context for teaching deliberately.
>
> —Jerome Bruner, *The Culture of Education*

For her senior thesis in communication, Carolyn wrote a more than forty-page study of Northwest Airlines' fifty-year campaign to promote their Asia-Pacific flights. She said that as a first-year student she could not have completed this final project. She would not have known how to formulate the problem, how to contact people from the company and get information, or how to analyze the information and not just report what they did. Having completed similar, shorter projects in courses in her major made her confident that she could take on this challenging writing task and "get the job done." Carolyn said that when she chose the public relations major she thought it was about being good with people. But, by her junior year, she realized, "Most of the job is how well you write and developing your writing skills."

It is beyond the scope of this study to explore in detail how students write in each of the disciplines represented. For one thing, there were only a few students from each field, and surely there is wide variation within each major. Instead, the study looked at similarities across disciplines, especially focusing on the ways students became more consciously aware of the disciplinary conventions in their major academic fields and more adept at negotiating these conventions. Papers in students' portfolios indicated their growing ability (in varying degrees) to deal with complexity and juggle the demands of academic writing including the following variables: employing appropriate genre and discourse conventions, locating and interpreting relevant sources, applying concepts from a discipline, developing evidence acceptable in the discipline, and organizing all of this information within a single coherent text. In interviews, students could explain specific strategies they used in writing and reasons for those strategies. Most came to see the requirements of their academic assignments as more than just "what the professor wanted" (though they did still encounter "picky" professors). Instead, they explained disciplinary conventions as necessary for writing in their academic fields and, perhaps, even useful in providing specific guidelines for specialized ways of writing.

It might be the case that students "pick up" the literacy strategies characteristic of their disciplines through reading texts in the field, listening and speaking in class, and unguided practice in writing. Certainly, much learning must occur in this way because, as Frank Smith (1982), Stephen Krashen (1984), and other literacy researchers have noted, the "rules" for writing are too many, too complex, and too little understood all to be explained consciously. However, students themselves pointed out important moments of transition when writing was consciously learned and they understood what was expected. As discussed previously, students did not always see these changes as improvements in their writing in general—they said that they already knew how to write—but as learning new ways of writing for specific purposes.

These new ways of writing were acquired as students spent more time in the academic "subcommunities" of their major disciplines. Though Pepperdine does not have an established writing-across-the-curriculum program, each of these subcommunities offers implicit or explicit instruction in writing through the strategies outlined in the quote by Bruner that prefaces this chapter. Each discipline, some more successfully than others, "models ways of doing or knowing, provides opportunities for emulation, offers running commentary, provides 'scaffolding' for novices, and even provides a good context for teaching deliberately" (Bruner, 1996, p. 21). As students take up the literacy tasks of their various disciplines, they write under the constraints imposed by classroom assignments and develop strategies for negotiating those constraints.

Those composition specialists who succumb to playing the missionary role in writing-across-the-curriculum programs may focus on providing tips from composition courses that could improve the teaching of writing in other academic disciplines. These strategies, however, are unlikely to be incorporated in new settings unless they fit the local environment and the ways that the subcommunity is already providing "scaffolding" for novices. Scaffolding gives learners the help they need to move from what they can already do to more complex tasks. Applebee (1984), for example, uses this term to refer to instructional support provided by the teacher but also warns that scaffolding need not be viewed reductively as simply a teacher-centered "lesson." Scaffolding also refers to how tasks can be structured and modeled and how the environment for working can be redesigned to support development. Scaffolding is the assistance that proficient members of a community offer to learners in Vygotsky's "zone of proximal development." What compositionists can do is assist the locals in other academic disciplines in identifying gaps in literacy development and suggest additional scaffolding to help students make transitions across those gaps. This process of assessing literacy development across disciplines is difficult because development occurs slowly over time and ways of "teaching" writing in other disciplines are often not explicitly articulated.

In this chapter, I want to focus again on "*what* is perceived, desired, feared, thought about, or acquired as knowledge" as students interact more closely with the local environments of their academic majors. Often to the frustration of faculty and students, the "skills" acquired in the first two years of college do not smoothly transfer to the more challenging tasks of specialized courses. Instead, in cultural psychologist Michael Cole's words, "mind emerges in the *joint* mediated activity of people," as students and faculty coconstruct the subcommunities in which learning occurs (p. 104). In this chapter, I look particularly at the scaffolding various disciplines provide to support student development in writing and analyze the roles of direct teaching, teacher and peer response, "hands-on" experience and apprenticeships, and the college-classroom context in changing how students write. The goal is to understand these writing environments from the participants' perspective, especially that of students, challenging again the fantasy that students should already know "how to write" for situations they have not yet encountered and demonstrating how their development continues, though not always in consistent ways apparent to individual faculty.

Direct Teaching of Writing, Research, and Ways of Knowing

Perhaps because of the perception that students should already know "how to write," writing courses beyond English I and II at Pepperdine are offered only in English and communication departments and are not required for all majors within these disciplines, so most students take no upper-division courses that focus solely on writing. Few students, then, follow a coherent sequence of courses designed to build advanced writing skills. The exceptions are students majoring within the department of communication and in the writing/rhetoric emphasis in English who are preparing for careers where writing is a primary job skill. Carolyn's public relations major is a good example of an academic subcommunity that has a clear plan for helping students make the transition from novice to experienced writers. From her first year, Carolyn was schooled in writing for the mass media, beginning with a general overview in Mass Communication 200. As a sophomore, she gained experience in editing and improving her writing. Because she failed by one point a standardized placement test of her grammar and editing skills, she was required to take Communication 200 where she was relentlessly drilled. While not all students in all majors would find this useful, Carolyn credited the class with teaching her not just rules but also how to use punctuation, varied sentence structure, and stylistic devices as "tools in order to make you a better writer; that's what we really learned about in that class." During the first semester of her junior year in Mass Communication 280, Writing for the Mass Media, Carolyn completed 33 different, short writing assignments in genres from news stories to advertisements and, in Public Relations 355, developed her first major public relations campaign, promoting the cancer fund-raising of her sorority. By the end of her senior year, she had completed, among other projects, a public service advertisement using computer graphics to warn against drunk driving, a public relations project for a charity event, a group project marketing bottled water, and her senior thesis, the more than forty-page study of Northwest Airlines. Though, as a senior, she was not sure she would actually work in public relations, Carolyn felt confident of her writing, of her ability to analyze new writing tasks and apply the mass-media strategies she had learned.

However, in most disciplinary subcommunities, unlike communication, writing serves as a tool to construct and interpret knowledge, but not as a major focus of instruction. Undergraduate majors like history and English literature, while heavily text based, do not explicitly prepare students for careers as writers, and there is no sequenced curriculum to develop writing skills. Other disciplines, like psychology, for example, emphasize research and application over writing as a primary focus. Yet, to look exclusively at the explicit teaching of "writing" in these disciplines is too narrow a focus. Many disciplines—including history, English, psychology (and several others) at Pepperdine—do deliberately teach literacy practices in research-methods courses. Though these are not "writing" courses, students identified these courses as places where they became more explicitly aware of the interplay between theory, research methods, and genre conventions. Elizabeth, for example, although she had completed several Great Books classes and English literature survey courses, was not aware that ways of writing about literature could represent different critical approaches. A required course in critical theory and literary research, which she initially failed and repeated in her senior year, helped her understand critical assumptions in the research she read and in her own writing. For Terri, learning to use primary sources was an important step in her history research course. Without this experience, she would not have been able to research and interpret nineteenth-century church newspapers for her senior thesis on the Millerite religious movement.

In psychology, Georgia at first resented her professor's insistence on correct American Psychological Association (APA) format and style in a research-methods course. Initially, she saw this as just another example of "giving the professor what she wants." By the end of the course, however, she reported that she felt much more confident in being able to write for a professional audience. Like other students, she came to see APA guidelines not as the idiosyncratic preferences of her professor but as a useful format for reporting information. Paul, another psychology major, mentioned research methods as just one course giving him practice in reading and writing APA-style studies. He suggested that students actually find writing easier when they "pick a major with a set style of writing" that they can use "when they go out into the world." Paul added, "If you're going to be a psychologist, you have to know how to write APA."

However, this deliberate instruction in research and writing still does not magically transform students into experts who can now write effectively on all topics within their disciplines. Most importantly, as students struggle with the complexity of new content-knowledge and genre conventions, they may lose track of the arguments they need to make in their writing. As a writing center director, I worked for several years with students from the psychology research-methods course. These students were given three pages of guidelines on which their papers were evaluated. As they wrote literature reviews, like Georgia's on childhood depression, students tried to apply these guidelines but often simply summarized a series of research articles. They either forgot, or found it too difficult, to construct an argument about childhood depression and to organize their research material to support this perspective. For many students, it required looking at model papers, critiquing drafts in peer groups and individual conferences, and then revising to help them make this next step toward analyzing, not just reporting, what they were learning. Research-methods courses provide a space in the curriculum for students to address explicitly the formation and communication of knowledge in their fields. However, learning disciplinary conventions is only the surface of what students need to know. Telling why something is important, and not just "dumping out your brain," as Julia called it, continues to be the most difficult task for students. Presumably, this analytical ability is emphasized in English I and II but not generalized to the new styles of writing in the major disciplines, where the content, methods, and style of analysis are quite different. In the writing center, the challenge is to "remind" students to "go back to" general notions of making assertions and supporting them, while fully understanding how these concepts play out in their fields. Responses from teachers and peers as well as grades suggest to students how well they are succeeding in the balancing act between appropriate content and form.

Responding to Student Writers: Comments and Grades

Student papers in the psychology research-methods class were rated, using each of the items listed on the three pages of guidelines. In addition, the professor wrote detailed notes on both the rating sheets and the students' texts. Because students could revise their work, some, like Georgia, felt more confident by the end of the course that they had mastered the basics of APA style and format. On the other hand, as Paul reviewed his portfolio, he explained that he never read the teacher's comments. He received 23 points out of 30 on his first draft and figured with his test scores he was sure of a "B" in the class. As he said, he was not motivated to revise.

The running commentary, in the form of comments, grades, and corrections, offered by teachers, and sometimes other learners, is a second strategy, in addition to deliberate teaching, used to instruct novices in the literacy practices of their disciplinary subcommunities. How students assess and make use of this commentary seems to be as context dependent as how teachers assess student writing. The teacher's commentary and the use students make of it cannot be understood outside the writing environment—the class, the content knowledge, the assignment, the teacher, and the student's perception of these—in which the commentary is embedded. While some commentary may seem overly detailed or too focused on minor errors from the perspective of compositionists, every type of comment seems to work with at least some students. Like student writing itself, commentary is, perhaps, best assessed in terms of the fit between the goals of the commentator, the text itself, and the response of the audience, in this case, the student learner.

Students, with limited time and many interests, are strategic about their uses of literacy. In general, they are as literate as they need to be to accomplish their own goals, including earning acceptable grades. In our study, students said they liked comments from teachers on their writing and that they usually read them. When there were no comments on their papers, they wondered if their professors had actually read their work. But grades, once again, functioned as important signals to students and influenced their response to comments. Students weighed the cost of spending time on a paper against the likely benefit of a better grade. For Paul, responding to three pages of comments meant a lot of work for a few more points on his paper and little improvement on his grade in the class. In addition to grades, students also considered the context of the class as a whole, especially how much they personally felt motivated by the content of the course and the teacher. Paul, who enjoyed theorizing, found his research-methods class mainly a matter of memorizing notes and textbook materials, something he could do without much effort. In keeping with his philosophy of being satisfied with a "good enough" grade point average and a good social life, Paul was not inspired to greater efforts by the teacher's detailed comments.

On the other hand, the commentary offered by grades can be a signal to students that they need to make changes in their writing, especially when they are also personally engaged by their courses and when the teacher points out specifically how they can improve their work. For example, Andrea explained that she felt unprepared for upper-division courses in political science, a major with only one or two required lower-division courses to prepare students for advanced work. After receiving "A's" in English I and II, she was dismayed by the low grades on her writing in three upper-division political science courses during the second semester of her sophomore year. When I asked if she could have been better prepared by

English I and II, she answered, "It's something you have to learn in poly sci. It's bad that you have to learn the hard way." Andrea, who was highly motivated by her political science courses, needed rapidly to acquire both content-knowledge and new ways of writing. Of her jurisprudence course, for example, she said, "I loved the class. That was the thing. I just couldn't understand why I was doing so horrible in the class." Her professor's detailed comments helped her to see what she could do differently. Her legal brief on the Supreme Court case, *Plyler v. Doe,* examined "Whether a state is obligated to provide a tuition free public education to children unlawfully present in the U.S." Her professor's comments combined encouraging praise with probing questions. For example, on page four of this eight-page paper, he wrote, "<u>Good</u> review of the applicability of E.P. [Equal Protection] clause to illegal immigrants. Brennan went on to demonstrate that the state could not legally restrict education to citizens. Why?" The grade of "79," a "C+," lower than Andrea expected, suggested that she needed a new approach for her political science papers. Most importantly, she said, she learned that she needed to read differently. While in the past in her reading and writing she had aimed at getting general ideas, what she called "the overall picture," now she realized that she needed to focus on specifics, that small details and facts were needed to explain that big picture.

In all of her major courses, Andrea continued to struggle to find a balance between the "what" and the "why" of her writing, between reporting information and analyzing it with sufficient depth. Could this process have been less painful? Andrea suggested that professors helped when they assigned several papers giving students a chance to improve gradually. Students helped themselves, she said, by "going in to see the professor and see what you're doing wrong." Despite practice and detailed feedback from her professors, Andrea progressed slowly. She said, professors "already expect you to be at a certain level," but she had to learn as she worked her way through each class. She summed up the story of development when she said, "I look back on my education at Pepperdine, and I wish I could have taken that class [jurisprudence] now. Because I am ready for it." Apparently college writing is another of life's catch-22's; you have to be ready before you can do it, but you can't get ready until you do it.

Grades and teacher comments, then, are read in context, a context not controlled solely by the teacher but coconstructed by the student's interests and experiences. Terri, turned off by "C's" in her English classes, and Deborah, who felt her teacher was biased, did not feel improved by their teachers' comments, no matter how extensive or well thought out. Some of the most effective feedback we observed in portfolios was in speech classes, where students explicitly coconstructed the commentary assessing their work. In these classes, students wrote self-assessments, received critiques from other students, and wrote responses to their teachers' comments. Students' written responses to teacher comments meant that the students actually read what the teacher wrote and had a chance to describe how they felt about their own work, what they saw as their own strengths and weaknesses. Standards of assessment for speech were clearly spelled out in check-sheets and then exemplified and negotiated over the course of several different assignments. Students were not just "giving the professor what she wants"; they played an active role in assessing their own progress in the course.

The weakest feedback to student writing was on those papers and projects that Julia described as follows: "Well, we turn them in at the end of the semester and then I don't know what happens to them." Surprisingly, when we in the portfolio project occasionally retrieved these projects from professors, we found they sometimes had comments written on them, comments students had never seen.

Responding to Student Writers: Correcting Errors, Revising Style

In addition to grades and general commentary, many student papers in the study were marked with detailed corrections in usage, punctuation, and style. While we did not systematically study the effects of these kinds of corrections, it is clear, again, that the way students take up corrections is dependent on the writing environment and the student's, as well as the teacher's, goals. Every type of correction seems to work for some students, but no one type works for every student. Despite teachers' complaints that students cannot spell or punctuate, the students in our study, in fact, did not make many basic errors in the conventions of written English, and many of the errors they did make could be attributed to their last-minute writing processes. Teacher corrections were more often addressed not to basic errors but to style, untangling vague or confusing sentences and modeling conventions of a specific academic discipline.

Randall, who graduated with a 3.23 GPA in biology, provides an example of typical "good enough" writing and some typical teacher response. As a preface to his web pages, Randall, in his senior year, wrote the following "Quote on Life": "Life is not about the accomplishments you can make and the number of letters after you [sic] name, its [sic] the people you were able to help along the way." Although the sentiment is admirable, I am sorely tempted to edit Randall's writing, which will appear in the public forum of a web site. When a colleague teaching business law at the University of California Los Angeles tells me that "students today" cannot write, her most damning piece of evidence is that they don't know the difference between "it's" and "its."

Randall's professors have certainly corrected his writing, especially to demonstrate stylistic choices appropriate to writing in science. Within academic disciplines, comments on style are another way of alerting students that they must change their "normal" way of writing. Randall's paper on "Density Control and Distribution of Great White Shark, *Carcharodon carcharias* Along the North American West Coast," written in the first semester of his senior year, was certainly more complex than his quote on life. His teacher corrected several items in Randall's first paragraph (see the following figure).

Throughout the paper, Randall was clearly trying to write in an appropriate scientific style. Although his sentences were sometimes vague and confusing, perhaps because he was trying to sound like a scientist, the only real "error" in his seven-page research report was a comma splice in a long and complicated sentence. His *conducted*

Many ~~Studies~~ involving interactions and distribution of sharks have long been ~~under~~— ~~way~~ in the last decade. Scientists struggle to gather data on these elusive, dangerous creatures in order to better understand their habits and life *histories* ~~patterns~~. The Great White shark, *Carcharodon carcharias*, which ranks as one of the most well-known and most dangerous of all sharks, has recently gathered special attention *why?* ~~in the pursuit of these~~ ~~patterns~~. Some of the many problems faced in studying white sharks include the ~~limited~~ *lack of* ~~attainable~~ *and attainable* data available, ~~to scientists~~ on their behaviors. Data on the white is limited to their (capture) and ~~its~~ (location) and to the observations of known white shark feeding *at site of capture?* grounds. Until recently scientists have only been able to gather data on white sharks through baited interactions in which sharks are brought close to a vessel to feed on a carcass.

What?
wt., size,
stomach
contents
? ? ?

professor acted as an editor, questioning unclear sentences and rewording convoluted ones. Randall got a grade of 9.5 out of 10, and the teacher commented, "Good paper. Nicely organized and focused. You need to work on explaining ideas more clearly." Randall, who said his hobbies were "surfing, surfing, surfing," had a strong personal interest in sharks and chose this paper as one of his best works to be included in his digital portfolio. While Randall did not revise this paper after it was graded or comment on the teacher's specific corrections, presumably, the comments indicated that he needed to continue his efforts to write appropriately for his discipline.

To some readers, certain kinds of surface errors, like Randall's disregard for the distinction between "its" and "it's," seem to stigmatize students as poor writers; yet, when I reviewed our study portfolios of work collected over four years, these errors seemed insignificant compared to the greater challenges that face students in writing critically about complex topics. Despite teacher concerns about commas and misspelled homonyms not caught by spell checkers, most of our study students made some but not many egregious surface errors even as first-year students, and they continued to make surface errors even as seniors. The weaknesses in their style and word choice are hard to separate from their difficulties in dealing with complex subject-matter and, also, the time pressures under which they worked.

On the other hand, extensive corrections at the sentence level can change students' writing when they are motivated to work on style and, especially, when they have opportunities to revise over several papers as Carolyn did in English II. Because surface errors do stigmatize students in the eyes of many readers, certainly, classes that focus specifically on writing, like English I and II, should spend time on producing edited final drafts as well as exploratory first drafts. Further, in majors like Carolyn's, public relations, where the goal is to produce professional writers, students can be systematically trained to be good editors. However, unless a discipline wants to put this emphasis on editing, students are, again, likely to be strategic about their literacy and less concerned about punctuation than they are about content. Susanna, a science major who actually was a very skilled writer, said "If you're real into science, you just don't want to sit there and memorize comma rules and stuff. I just have no interest in that. And so, I figure if it's real important, an editor is going to be looking at it, and that's kind of their job." Almost every professor in Sarah's major, English, wrote on her essays the reminder that "the comma goes inside the quotation marks." I counted at least 10 examples of this comment in her portfolio. Yet Sarah always got "A's" and "B's" on her otherwise thoughtful essays and sprinkled her commas inside or outside of quotation marks, seemingly as the mood struck her. Allison, a friend of Sarah's, working for the portfolio project as a student assistant, told me that Sarah was "too intellectual" to be bothered by such minor details. Terri, as discussed earlier, agreed that teachers' rewritten versions of her sentences might be more correct but she did not internalize them. She said she continued to write as she spoke, that is, with just a very few markers of an African-American English vernacular typical of urban Los Angeles.

In some ways, the time and effort professors put into corrections may serve a symbolic, if not a practical, purpose. These corrections indicate that the professor pays attention to editing. Leslie was impressed that her political science professor took the time to write a typed, full-page response to each of the 30 students in the class. After commenting on her content, sources, and analysis, he noted a problem with her use of "which" rather than "that." He wrote, "I may be trying to fight a losing battle on this latter point, but I take my cue from Strunk and White's *The Elements of Style,* which provides a logical (and comprehensible) distinction between the two." While Leslie admitted she still didn't really understand the distinction the professor was making between "which" and "that," she took his comment as a sign that he had read her work and cared about her progress as a writer. If faculty wish to have more than a symbolic effect on student writing, they might first rethink how much emphasis they really want to put on style and editing and then provide the scaffolding to support this emphasis rather than relying primarily on corrections on completed work. Discussing models of writing, providing guidelines for editing, adjusting grading practices to reflect editing concerns, organizing classroom workshops, encouraging revision, and giving multiple assignments that require students to apply what they have learned are all rather homely but effective strategies.

Throughout, however, faculty need to sort out distinctions between errors and the specific stylistic conventions they want students to learn in their discipline and between sentence-level problems and the much more difficult tasks of researching, reporting, and analyzing information. By focusing too much on the sentence-level skills, which they think students should already know, faculty may miss the real problems students have in learning to write in new and more complex ways.

Response from Peers

Luckily, faculty need not be the only teachers for students. In addition to the deliberate instruction provided by teachers, Bruner (1996) points out "that learners 'scaffold' for each other as well." This is another area we did not explore in-depth, but students in our study provided hints of its importance. Interviews with students suggested that much informal tutoring goes on in residence halls and student apartments. At the beginning of his junior year, Paul took an upper-division history course on colonial and revolutionary America because he needed "extra units," and two of his roommates were in the class. His final course paper on "The French and Indian War at Quebec" got high marks from the professor, and although this was the only history paper in Paul's portfolio, it seemed quite appropriate in form, style, and supporting evidence. I asked Paul, a psychology major, how he knew how to write a "history" paper. As he explained his process, it was clear that he drew on his Great Books experience in selecting a topic, skimming sources for appropriate quotes and supporting details, and constructing an essay combining narrative and analysis of events in Quebec in 1759. In addition, Paul also turned to his roommate, a history major, as a source of information. The roommate was able to explain and check his overall format and his citation style, including the use of footnotes.

Teachers can, of course, build on this informal process of students teaching students. In Deborah's senior-year telecommunications course in broadcasting and programming, she learned from the teacher's feedback but also from in-class critiques where students assessed each other's work. Unlike her English I class, where she felt locked in an individual struggle with her professor over her ideas, in this telecommunications course, the students helped evaluate each other's projects. Deborah saw examples of good and bad techniques in their work, and she felt comfortable imitating their good ideas in her own projects. This was perhaps easier for her as a senior in a subcommunity with what she saw as the shared professional values of her telecommunications major rather than in the more heterogeneous classroom of English I during her first year. As part of the developmental process, Deborah was sorting through and adopting criteria to assess her own process. Deborah's resistance as a first-year student may seem discouraging to a teacher, but, as a senior, Deborah was articulate and self-aware. She used the critiques of other students and the teacher to improve her work, and by contrasting her projects to those of others, she said she came to recognize her own style.

Study groups are another way students learn from each other. Terri usually struggled alone with her course work and job responsibilities. She explained that professors seemed to assume she understood what they expected and added, "Maybe everybody else knows, but I didn't know." She said that because of her work schedule and her experience at an urban high school, where "students never talked to teachers," she did not talk to her teachers, use resources like the writing center, or study with other students. In her senior year, professors coteaching an American legal history course organized the class into study groups and required that students attend once a week. For Terri, this was an enlightening experience. Although she could not say exactly what information she learned in her study group, just talking about ideas helped her to be more successful on her written essay exams. Paul, who went to a private high school and stressed the importance of having a "social life," expected to get help from his teachers and his friends. But not all students will seek out this kind of support. Professors need to structure opportunities, perhaps required conferences and study groups, where all students can talk through what they do and do not understand, an important corollary to learning from written texts.

Learning Through Experience

The "hands-on" art history paper and other similar projects rated highly with students as they looked back on their experience in general-education courses. The "hands-on" experience continued to be a significant way of learning as students entered specialized subcommunities both outside and inside the classroom. One of the questions we asked students in yearly assessments was what important learning experiences were *not* represented in their portfolios. What would we not know about them from looking just at their portfolios? Carolyn pointed out that her experience as president of the Panhellenic Council of Greek Organizations on campus had been as important to her as her classroom learning experiences in public relations. The council was formed in reaction to a movement by the university to ban all fraternities and sororities. Instead, Greek organizations were given the opportunity to reform unacceptable practices in choosing members, hazing initiates, encouraging binge drinking, and other negative behaviors. As the first president of the new council, Carolyn conducted meetings, gave many speeches, and wrote extensively—letters, memos, guidelines, and plans for events. As she said, "I couldn't come off sounding like a babbling idiot. I had to use those skills that I had learned in my classes." In turn, she brought her experiences back to the classroom, when she developed projects for her public relations courses based on sorority charitable fund-raising activities.

In the communication program, with its emphasis on career training, "hands-on" experiences and internships gave students opportunities to test their classroom learning. Deborah was perhaps more open to critiques in her telecommunications classes because she had first-hand experience with how television news shows are actually produced. After working for the campus TV station, she had internships with two local television stations. Her first internship was primarily clerical, but at the second, she was mentored by the manager of the assignment desk and had the opportunity to write news copy. Another measure of students' development is their ability to handle these professional assignments. Clearly, their classroom experience helps. Natalie, interning at Nickelodeon television, credited a public relations class with teaching her to write under pressure. Initially, she said she disliked the course, where students were given assignments that had to be completed before the end of class. However, it gave her enough confidence not to panic when she had similar deadlines at Nickelodeon. Nonetheless, in these new roles, again, students needed some time and experience to adjust to new forms of writing. Natalie pointed out that every organization has its own style. She looked at models and got feedback from her supervisors to learn how to write press releases specifically for Nickelodeon.

While not directly focused on writing, Andrea was able to redefine her career goals during two summer internships in Washington,

D.C. A stint in the White House legal counsel office convinced her that she did not want the kind of high-pressure government or corporate job she had initially desired. Instead, a second internship working for a nonprofit legal-reform organization brought her in contact with people who could not afford more expensive counsel. After that experience, she decided she would like to be "some kind of advocate," especially for women and children. When I asked about reading and writing in these jobs, her role was routine, reading letters and sometimes writing replies using boilerplate responses. However, these internships increased her interest and effort in courses on jurisprudence and constitutional law processes.

Terri, as a history major, was able to earn money and follow some of her own interests in her job at the Skirball Cultural Center, an educational center and museum in Los Angeles that traces the history of the Jewish people. Terri had turned away from writing about issues of race because, as an African American woman, she found them too personal and painful and had not felt supported in her early efforts in English classes. Terri reported that she found "the perfect topic" at the Skirball. She could identify with the oppression of the Jewish people, had excellent opportunities for research, and could explore her interest in civil-rights issues in a form other than personal narrative. These interests came together in her paper on "The Maryland Jew Bill."

Apprenticeships can occur on as well as off campus. Susanna, a sports medicine major who wanted to be a doctor, is the best example in our study of this kind of apprenticeship learning and is a model of development nurtured over four years. Susanna illustrates the reciprocal nature of development, the interplay between the individual and the environment. Neither is static; the individual shapes her environment as the environment shapes her. I knew Susanna rather well because she was one of the students who spent a semester studying with me in Pepperdine's program in Florence, Italy. She came to Pepperdine from a small, private high school in Michigan, graduating with a 4.0 GPA. She projected those stereotypical traits fairly certain to gain favor in the classroom; Susanna was likely to impress teachers as bright, mature, and hardworking.

Perhaps for this reason, Susanna was asked as a first-year sports medicine major to attend a weekly seminar in which her professors were discussing a new research project. Susanna, shaping her own environment, accepted. She read research reports and learned that even articles in the *New England Journal of Medicine* can be critiqued. During that first year, she attended the American Conference of Sports Medicine in San Diego where, she said, "I had no idea what any of these people were talking about when I would sit in these lectures. . . . it was more like let's go to San Diego and have fun for the weekend." Studying in Florence, she missed the conference her sophomore year, but, she said, "And then junior year I went and it was starting to all click in. But by the time I went senior year, I could understand everything they were talking about." In addition to attending sessions at the conference in her senior year, Susanna also did a PowerPoint poster presentation, answering questions, for two hours, based on knowledge drawn from research done collaboratively with a professor and another student.

Susanna could explain, in detail, how she developed the skills to make this professional presentation on the "Effect of Gender on Myocardial Work during Progressive Treadmill Exercise." From her first year, three professors that she worked with most closely emphasized research and writing. Especially in her junior and senior years, she had extensive practice in writing case studies, lab reports, and scientific research papers. For example, in her course on motor control, she said she spent five to seven hours researching and writing up labs that were due almost every week. Although she said it was frustrating that she could not often get "A's" on these reports, she did get feedback and comments, so she could see improvement over time. According to Susanna, all three professors in her major seemed consistently to expect the same kind of writing, appropriate for journals in the field. Susanna participated in research projects with two of these professors and did her own research along with two other students for the third professor. By her senior year, she was working as a volunteer at Santa Monica–UCLA Hospital and wrote two case studies of patients that were rated "100/excellent" by her teacher.

Susanna is the kind of student who is likely to thrive in almost any educational environment. However, her collaboration with her professors, her apprenticeship as part of a professional community, provided a scaffolding that allowed her to produce work more complex than she would have been able to accomplish on her own. Service learning, internships, and other "hands-on" experiences give students another standard, outside the classroom, with which they can measure their own development. Often, we reserve these experiences for our best students, those we perceive as most amenable to our instruction. In fact, most students could benefit from structured opportunities to learn from those experiences that extend their in-class learning.

Constraints on Writing

No matter how much teaching, commentary, and support students receive, at some point each must pick up a pen or sit in front of a computer and actually produce a written text. Professors may take any one text as a measure of a student's general writing ability, but each text also reflects the context in which it is written, the ways in which a student's performance is constrained as well as enabled by the circumstances of writing for the college classroom.

As I discussed previously, from the student's perspective, the greatest constraint is giving professors what they want. Later in their careers, however, students may accept these constraints as necessary to conform to the standards of their academic discipline and the professional community they wish to join. Do these constraints act as a straightjacket on student writing, preventing them from developing ideas outside disciplinary boundaries? On the one hand, many students in our study explained that, to some extent, as juniors and seniors they were able to bring their own voices back into their disciplinary writing, to choose topics of personal interest, to evaluate the "facts" they were reporting, and to include their own opinions. This was true in science and the social sciences as well as in communication and the humanities. On the other hand, in our study, while students complained about grades and individual "picky" professors, we rarely saw students challenging more global disciplinary expectations. Deborah, for example, in her senior year, expressed reluctance to challenge her professors directly, "I study the comments that the professors make and try to adjust as best I can—even if it means writing down what they want to hear instead of what I believe. This is probably bad, but I have an academic scholarship to take care of and grades mean a lot." What will this mean if Deborah pursues her career in telecommunications? Will she and her peers change television news or, as seems more likely, accommodate to current practices? The negative effect of training students to imitate the literacy practices of academic subcommunities or the workplace is that students come to regard these ways of knowing and writing as "objective" standards, the way one must perform if one wants to be a scientist, psychologist, lawyer, English professor, or producer of television news.

While students complained that they didn't understand disciplinary conventions or found them foreign to their "normal" ways of writing, they never objected that the conventions themselves might be wrong, that the standard could change, not the student. Perhaps, because academic disciplines themselves are not monolithic, students find enough different perspectives to begin questioning generic standards and formats. Andrea, through her internships, was able to contrast being a lawyer at the White House with being a lawyer at a nonprofit legal-aid agency. Natalie, as an intern at Nickelodeon, learned about commercial and ethical conflicts in developing children's programming. Paul wrote a paper comparing different approaches to psychotherapy and explained which he would incorporate into his own practice. Although he worried that he got "graded down" because he did not agree with his professor's ideas about counseling, he did have to sort through several competing perspectives. However, while I know students and professors discuss ethical issues and disciplinary conflicts in their classes, the primary focus of most academic majors seems to be preparing students for jobs and graduate school, turning students into mini-professionals, who can read, write, and speak like their professors. Because disciplines are so specialized with a sense of so much knowledge to be imparted, there is little room for leisurely contemplation of how knowledge and experience might be constructed otherwise.

This sense of too much to learn, too much to do, is a major constraint on student performance. When professors judge writing ability and learning based on individual student texts, they most often are assessing writing produced under tight time constraints. It should come as no surprise to anyone who has been on a college campus that most student writing is completed very close to a deadline set by the professor, rarely more than a day or two, often the night before the work must be turned in. Both Carolyn and Sarah, who were quite successful in their classroom writing, reported waiting until the end of the semester to write their senior theses. They had researched, made notes, and thought about their papers, but did not begin drafting. Sarah explained that she had written almost every one of her "A" English papers the day before it was due. Being able to write more quickly can be a sign of progress to students. While Randall said that as a first-year student it took him five days to write a science research paper, he reported as a senior that, after doing the necessary research, he could write a paper in two days.

In interviews, students always apologized for not spending more time on their writing. They felt like they should have begun writing sooner, but they didn't. However, although they didn't begin actually drafting their papers early, they did start the writing process. These writers had learned to manage their time sufficiently, so that they began going to the library, conducting research, reading, thinking, meeting with other students for group projects, interviewing, and generally gathering material before they actually began "writing." Their difficulty was in setting aside a block of time to focus on producing a coherent text. Like many other writers, they could not have kept track of what they were thinking and writing if they had had to write in short bursts, say one page written during one hour a day for a week instead of seven pages written in five or six hours in front of the computer. These students, like other writers, looked for some kind of flow in order to produce coherent work.

They needed some uninterrupted hours to draft their writing. Theoretically, they should have had plenty of time available, since they spent relatively few hours a week actually in class. However, their time seemed fragmented, especially as they juggled their personal lives and the requirements of several different courses. It took the pressure of a deadline to push aside other commitments and make room for the hours needed for writing.

How do students manage their time? During their first year at Pepperdine, 28 students in our original study group kept time logs of their activities for a week. These logs were analyzed by natural science professor Laurie Nelson. She found that these students spent a mean of 16.7 hours in class and 23 hours outside of class on academic activities. Sleep took up 54.4 hours, the combined categories of social and other leisure activities accounted for 31.5 hours, personal affairs, such as showering and eating (which could also be counted as a social activity), took 23.1, and the remainder of students' time was spent in employment (6.2 hours), sports, campus activities, religious activities, and visiting their families and friends at home. While we did not repeat the time logs in subsequent years of the study, this gave us at least one picture of student life. My impression is that the time spent in employment or internships increased for most students after the freshman year. Even in students' first year, the amount of time spent studying outside of class showed a great deal of variation. With the exception of one student who reported 78 hours of study (a major project to complete?), the range during a midsemester week, not final exams, was from about 5 hours to about 40.

Certainly, some students had much less time than others. During his senior year, Paul worked almost 40 hours a week as a manager in a video store. As a senior, Terri put in 30 hours at the Skirball Cultural Center. Terri had worked three jobs the summer after her sophomore year to buy a car so she would not have to take a bus to school and work. She earned so much money that her financial aid was cut, necessitating working more hours during her junior and senior years. She said, "Professors may think I'm not trying, but I am."

Professors, however, may wish that students would reallocate some hours from the social and leisure categories to invest more time in academic projects. Students often frustrate professors' efforts to get them started early on projects. In the psychology research-methods class, students had a draft deadline and the opportunity to revise before a final draft was due. While this did get them started on their research, many drafts were haphazard. Since this was not the "real" deadline, some students reported that they hastily produced a few pages for an in-class writing workshop and planned to write their "real" papers later. While students' final papers improved through discussing the ideas in even these very rough drafts, professors need to structure class activities carefully, if they really want to impact students' usual writing processes. Paul, you may remember, was satisfied with the "good enough" grade he could earn in psychology research methods without revision. That might be acceptable to both the student and the professor. However, if the professor wanted to push Paul a bit more, she might give the draft only part of the points for the assignment and reserve additional points for a revised final draft. Students need to be strategic in the management of their time and will weigh the cost of improvements, especially improvements as mandated by the teacher, against benefits they will gain from additional work.

From the students' perspective, professors may expect too much for the time allowed to complete complex assignments. During her first year, Andrea was frustrated by being asked to research her family history and relate it to library sources in only a few weeks. In-class essays sometimes seem to ask students to do the impossible in one or two hours. For Carolyn's art history class, an essay exam question read, "Twentieth-century art reflects the problems of our age. Discuss." The following semester, in a humanities class, she was asked, "Expand on the theme: The Romantic Hero. Give examples from art, music, and literature." To be successful, students learn not to address these assignments in too much depth. They have to do work that is just good enough for the time allotted. These are not necessarily bad assignments as long as professors make reasonably clear what they expect in the time allowed. Vanessa, with a family history perhaps more accessible than Andrea's, loved the family-history project, and Carolyn wrote neat, coherent, informative little essays for those in-class exams in art history and the humanities. However, while any one of these assignments may be useful, the overall picture of student learning can seem rushed and fragmented. Again, it can seem that students are getting a kind of workplace training, a workplace, even in academia, where the ability to juggle many different tasks under time constraints is highly valued. Far from being an ivory tower of leisurely contemplation, college continues to sort students for future jobs, putting special value on time management.

Student Writing Strategies

In the context of social life and job responsibilities vying with academic demands for time each week, students struggle with problems familiar to most writers. At the beginning of their senior year, 16 students in our study filled out questionnaires, describing the difficulties they experienced in writing and the strategies they used to overcome these difficulties. Only one student mentioned "basic" writing problems. Stephen wrote that his greatest difficulties were spelling and conclusions, problems he addressed by getting help from his professors and other students and using a spell-check program. Almost half of the students (7) located their difficulties with the audience, with writing to meet the demands of their academic readers. The other half (8) located the problem in themselves as writers, in trying to draft in words the ideas they wanted to express. This difference in perspective in our small sample does not seem to correlate with students' majors or their success as academic writers and perhaps simply reflects the two perspectives—audience and self—that every writer must maintain, sometimes focusing on one, sometimes on the other. Those focusing on audience mentioned again adjusting to what the professor expected, meeting requirements for length, and writing in different styles according to assignments, for example, "creative" versus "objective" writing. Strategies for overcoming these difficulties included studying professors' comments, looking at models, getting opinions from others, brainstorming, outlining, and, in Allison's case, screaming and crying "until my head is clear." Vanessa summed up the writing-for-the-audience problem when she wrote, "I have difficulty in writing when I am assigned something without clear expectations. . . . I am better when I have something specific to write about."

Andrea tried to bridge the gap between self and audience. She reported a typical problem for writers, "Sometimes I cannot find the appropriate word to convey what I am trying to say or what I want the reader to get out of my writing. It is also difficult, at times, to phrase a sentence to mean what I want it to mean." Other students echoed this difficulty in finding the right words to get down on paper their ideas and opinions. They expressed difficulties in getting started writing, organizing, being focused, being descriptive but not repetitive, and wandering off topic. Sarah noted, "My most often encountered difficulty is clarity and simplicity." Some of these students were explorers. Their strategies were, in the case of Paul, "I tend to just start writing," and, for Georgia, "I like to explore and play with my words and research." In contrast, Elizabeth's strategy was "I try to focus in on exactly what I'm trying to say and exclude all else. Often I do this by formulating a very precise thesis and an outline to follow before I actually begin writing in paragraph form." Susanna also emphasized, "Organization! I try to write a strong main statement & [sic] then follow that by back-up statements & examples until the statement is entirely picked apart & proven, followed by a memorable conclusion." Despite the emphasis placed on revision in composition courses, only two students mentioned rewriting as a strategy they used, and Carolyn, trying to avoid revision, said she tried to fit in new words, phrases, or ideas that came to her while she was writing, rather than go back and change what she had already written.

Although students could often identify their own writing problems and effective writing strategies, knowing what to do was not the same as knowing how to do it. Terri pointed out how solving one problem could cause others. Her biggest problem was writing long papers. She said that she had developed a system, "I divide it into sections or mini chapters [sic] and work on them independently. This is the only way I can be concise and thorough." Then, her problem became one of creating transitions between these sections. This lack of transitions was apparent in her senior thesis as was some difficulty in keeping track of exactly what argument she wanted to make. And yet, clearly, she had developed over four years a much greater facility in handling a complex topic in greater depth and detail and in a style and format appropriate to her history major. When we judge the individual written texts students produce, we may lose sight of the students themselves as writers struggling with the same problems that all writers, including ourselves, face, and we may forget how many years of experience it takes to learn new strategies. Sarah had only three common sense words to explain how she overcame difficulties in writing, words which I will transcribe exactly as she wrote them, "Practice . . . practice . . . practice!"

Performing New Roles

When the students in this study, after four years in college looked back through their portfolios, first-year composition seemed very far away. The lessons that these students had learned in English I and II were subsumed in the much larger experience of making the long transition from being novice college writers to becoming more mature, young adults able to perform in a variety of new roles. From this longitudinal perspective, I repeat the admonition from chapter 1 that composition specialists should take first-year courses seriously, but I will add, again, the dispensation that we should not take these courses too seriously, especially if we expect them permanently to transform students' writing, writing processes, or thinking in only one or two semesters. The *how* of writing cannot be separated from the *what*. The *what*—in Bronfenbrenner's (1979) terms "*what* is perceived, desired, feared, thought about, or acquired as knowledge"—is developed slowly over time and "changes as a function of a person's exposure to and interaction with the environment" (p. 9).

Students cannot write expertly as social scientists, psychologists, or literary critics in English I or II, not only because they lack experience with academic genres but also because they lack basic concepts and content knowledge that are essential for critical analysis. As Andrea said about writing for her jurisprudence course, "It's something you have to learn in poly sci." While beginning composition may introduce students to various social issues or cultural studies, as well as to ways of writing, I am skeptical of claims for English I and II courses that supposedly revolutionize students' thinking. Students do not become more critical simply by *thinking* about a topic. Writers need concepts and knowledge to think with. While students in this study certainly brought concepts and knowledge with them to college, the *what* of their thinking was altered by being immersed in new academic subcommunities. The study students could explain more clearly the perspectives they learned in their major disciplines than they could recall the lessons from composition courses taken in the first few months of their college careers.

Whether their learning was planned or unplanned, students in this study did learn new ways of writing across the curriculum. These ways of writing were embedded in larger literacy tasks—how to formulate a problem, how to get information, how to analyze that information. Andrea discovered that in order to *write* more effectively in political science, she had to learn to *read* differently. Carolyn, in public relations, learned how to contact the right people and ask the right questions. Natalie was able to apply general writing skills from her communication courses to her internship at Nickelodeon, analyzing models and using feedback from her supervisors to write appropriate press releases.

Although, as Andrea said, professors "already expect you to be at a certain level," the study students continued to develop as they transitioned into new roles and new environments. Each academic subcommunity provided scaffolding to support that development. Research-methods courses were effective places in the curriculum where writing was placed in the larger context of how the discipline constructs and reports knowledge, though, again, students hardly emerged as experts after a single semester. Grades on written work indicated to students how well they were acquiring the knowledge and discourse conventions of their disciplines. Comments and corrections on individual student texts were part of a larger "running commentary" demonstrating how learners might improve their performance. This commentary continued in classrooms and conferences and outside of class as learners helped each other figure out what was expected. The *what* of this commentary varied: from questions of critical analysis, to examples of disciplinary style, to corrections of basic errors. Students needed to decide for themselves how to use this commentary, unless further direction was supplied by the teacher.

Students do best what they do most, and those who chose majors specializing in writing, of course, received the most explicit instruction in writing. These students, like Carolyn, demonstrate that very careful editing, which preoccupies many teachers, is actually a rather specialized skill that can be taught with sufficient time and interest from the student and teachers. However, few disciplines or students would care to invest the time in editing that is expected in communication, where it is considered a primary job skill. Instead, students, and many teachers, are strategic about their literacy and aim for work that is "good enough," given the time constraints of classroom assignments and the goals of most disciplines to produce knowledgeable practitioners, but not necessarily professional writers.

When students faced major projects in writing across the disciplines, they struggled with the same concerns that trouble most writers, including professors. How does one carve out enough time for writing? Will this writing satisfy the audience? How can I find what I want to say and organize all of it in a coherent text? At other times, for students, their writing was a peripheral issue, not a major concern, as in Andrea's internships in Washington, where writing followed a prepackaged boilerplate format. While she was not practicing her "writing," certainly she gained valuable "hands-on" experience in problem posing and problem solving in two very different kinds of law offices. The writing of the study students across the disciplines did become more diverse and more complex during their years in college, but it was not the only measure of their learning.

5 / A Concluding Look at Development

Strict cause-effect relationships do not explain development
which entails the emergence of novel forms and functions
among people and their worlds.

—Michael Cole, *Cultural Psychology*

Understanding the work that we and our students do requires multiple perspectives, sometimes looking closely at specific reading and writing tasks but often stepping back to examine the longer process of development in which those tasks are embedded. Teachers rarely have the opportunity to follow students' development over time. Like proverbial blind men examining an elephant, professors tend to describe student literacy in terms of the one part they happen to get a hold on in their classes.

In the previous chapters, I looked across our study group of 20 students to analyze some of the ways their writing development was supported or constrained in their general education courses, their academic majors, and experiences outside the classroom. Here, I want to summarize our study conclusions focusing particularly on the role of first-year composition in writing development, the desirability of upper-level writing requirements, and on writing assessment. The last section of this chapter offers recommendations for instruction that supports student development.

Our study challenges the myth that even students who by most traditional measures would be considered "prepared" for college "can't write" and shows that the problems students face in academic writing are not primarily grammatical. It demonstrates that college writers who may be proficient in constructing simple reports or arguments will struggle with tasks that require more complex analysis and methods of presentation. However, it is in struggling with these tasks that they develop new skills. College faculty members can support novice writers in these periods of transition as students work out the strategies they need to take on new roles as writers.

The Role of First-Year Writing Courses

From our study, what can we conclude about the role of the ubiquitous, required first-year composition course in developing the proficiency in writing presumed to be useful in college or the workplace? Sharon Crowley (1998) and others have argued that the almost universally required composition course is so fraught with theoretical and practical problems that it ought to be entirely eliminated, replaced with writing electives that students can choose if they need them.

However, based on the experience of our study students, I would argue that institutions which require a core of general education courses should continue to require a one-semester writing course. Such a course serves a useful, albeit limited, purpose as a transition from high school and other previous writing experiences to writing in the university.

As Crowley argues and our research supports, there is no such entity as the generic academic essay. However, much of the writing our students collected in their portfolios does reflect some general academic expectations that run counter to many high school students' belief that a five-paragraph essay supported by general, often personal, reasons and examples will serve for most writing purposes. Students' "normal" ways of reading and writing, acquired through popular culture as well as through schooling, are challenged as they move into a new setting. In college, they must learn some new "basic skills," including reading and evaluating difficult texts that offer diverse viewpoints on complex issues, locating and then making sense of the overwhelming volume of information available through paper and digital sources, integrating new knowledge with personal experience and values, understanding and employing the conventions of new genres of writing, and writing as an "expert" for an often critical audience. These skills are reflected in students' writing across disciplines, from Randall's biology research report on sharks to Andrea's analysis of a Supreme Court case to Carolyn's fictitious fund-raising speech by Elizabeth Dole.

Students also point to the value across the curriculum of more homely skills, like finding an appropriate organizational structure and paragraphing, using transitions, developing some kind of controlling idea, constructing introductions and conclusions, and improving style and editing. Though there is no one generic essay form across the curriculum, many assignments and essay tests in general education courses and across disciplines do call for a thesis-driven analysis or argument supported by appropriate evidence. And this type of argument is also useful as a form of public discourse to debate civic issues. Beyond this general format, students need the rhetorical skill to analyze new writing situations and adapt to differing genre conventions. They need, like Andrea for example, to be able to adapt that more generic essay by recognizing that political science requires more factual and detailed analysis than what is generally expected in first-year courses.

Presumably, students could acquire all these skills "on-the-job" in discipline-specific courses; however, because the composition course is less concerned with "covering" subject matter, it can better provide a space early in the college experience for students to step back and focus directly on their own literacy development. From a developmental perspective, it makes sense to create such a space, where students can take stock of the literacy skills they have already acquired, encounter new expectations, and expand their repertoires without the added requirement of learning at the same time extensive new subject matter, as they will in more discipline specific courses.

Although students value learning specific literacy skills, developing metacognitive awareness is equally valuable. As Jerome Bruner (1996) argues, in subcommunities that specialize in learning, experienced practitioners and peers can help the student "to achieve full mastery by reflecting . . . upon how she is going about her job and how her approach can be improved" (64). First-year composition courses with an emphasis on rhetorical analysis and the processes of reading and writing and with teachers who are skilled in this type of analysis are especially appropriate places for this kind of reflection. A focus on developing metacognitive awareness as well as developing new writing skills is as useful for students who already know "how to write" as it is for less well-prepared writers. Without such awareness, "good" writers may find it especially difficult to change writing strategies that have worked for them in the past.

To truly reflect the diversity and difficulty of literacy tasks students are likely to encounter across the curriculum, most composition courses could be more challenging than they are now and could provoke even more conflict, both within the student and within the classroom. As Marilyn Sternglass (1997) points out in her study at The City College of The City University of New York, even students who are less experienced writers can develop the critical literacy skills necessary to succeed in college, if they are given sufficient time and support, and she urges that these students be challenged by complex literacy tasks from the beginning of their first composition courses, since these are the kinds of tasks they must learn to negotiate across disciplines.

Based on what we have learned from our longitudinal study, I have revised my own first-year writing course and, currently, as director of composition, I encourage other teachers to make similar changes. From their first assignments, students work with multiple texts, written in differing forms and offering different perspectives. A recent textbook by Charles Cooper and Susan MacDonald (2000), *Writing the World,* provides a good, prepackaged example of this type of assignment. Readings about gender and communication contrast popular perspectives like John Gray's *Men Are from Mars, Women Are from Venus* with more scholarly work done by Deborah Tannen and academic critiques from Katha Pollitt and Senta Troemel-Ploetz. Students struggle with the difficult task of evaluating so many different perspectives, especially those that may conflict with their own beliefs about gender. On a practical level, they struggle with how to construct an argument that won't fall neatly into a thesis-and-three-supporting-ideas format. And, often, they don't do this very well.

But here is where longitudinal research gives first-year students and their teachers a dispensation. Students do not have to "master" all aspects of academic writing; they need only to begin. They will spend years developing new ways of writing. This is not to say that "skills" don't matter. As in most composition courses, we spend much of our time looking at student papers and discussing how they might be more effective. Our study students especially valued this focus on their own writing and on specific suggestions about how their writing could be better. But we also have freedom to experiment. Students practice rhetorical analyses of different genres of writing in magazines and newspapers and try their hand at adapting one of their early academic essays for a different purpose and audience. A student, for example, may take her earlier work on gender and communication and use this information to write a self-help column for a teen magazine. Again, we are not interested in "mastering" journalistic writing but in "learning how to learn," in learning how to adapt writing for different contexts. In addition, we learn something about how the discourses of popular culture are constructed, how they may be misleading, and why they may not be successful in academic settings.

Based primarily on our study students' emphasis on the importance of "hands-on" learning, learning outside the classroom, I have also added a service-learning component to my English I course. As we research and write about issues in education, students work in local schools and tutoring programs. While the whole area of service and experiential learning deserves volumes on its own, (see, for example, Adler-Kassner, Crooks, and Watters, 1997), I can say here that from the perspective of literacy development, working outside the classroom does add a new element to students' repertoire. Though they are not writing for the schools in which they are working (another option), they are integrating observation and interviews with text-based research, again expanding their perception of the issues and of what is possible in their own research and writing.

Of course, because we are interested in development over time, students in English I and II keep portfolios of their writing, frequently assess their own work, and revise their writing over the course of the semester. In our longitudinal study, students reported that one of the reasons they stayed with the research project was because they valued having a record of their college experience in the form of their paper and, later, digital portfolios. These students enjoyed discussing the changes they observed in their own work. As experiments inevitably change the subjects of an experiment, students became more aware of their own development as they examined their own work and verbalized what they felt they were learning. Such metacognitive awareness helps promote further learning.

Focusing on first-year writing courses as a point of transition, not a final destination or a detour to fix literacy problems before students begin their real journey, means that many types of courses can be effective as long as they truly challenge students to move beyond their comfort zones and solve problems that are just beyond their reach. As I discussed in chapter 3, at Pepperdine we have experimented successfully with several kinds of special interest English I and English II courses, including sections focused on women's studies, ecology, service learning and social justice, the civil-rights movement, film, popular culture, and political issues, among other topics. We advertise these sections to incoming students who can choose a special emphasis or a more generic course. Through linked assignments, the special emphasis classes help students build content as well as process knowledge in order to write more complex critical analyses, though the focus of the course is always meant to stay on students' literacy, not on "covering" content. Some of the special emphasis sections also explicitly aim to change students' values as well as their writing, but again their influence is likely to be transitional. Some students will continue to follow an interest emphasized in English I or II, like Andrea, for example, who took as many courses as she could in African American studies. Others will continue to be involved in service to the community or women's issues on campus. Some will silently or not so silently resist, like Deborah, who felt her conservative values were under attack. For most, however, this one semester in their first year is certainly not a life-changing experience and becomes just one piece of the larger picture they construct from their personal experiences and classroom learning over four years.

Adding an Upper-Level Writing Requirement

In addition to a one semester first-year writing course, we have recommended, based on our longitudinal study, that Pepperdine, like many other universities, add an upper-level writing requirement to focus on writing in a student's major discipline. This requirement is satisfied at other institutions through writing-intensive courses or specific advanced writing courses. We found that the research and writing courses that some of our study students took in their major disciplines, for example, in psychology and history, were quite effective in making explicit the often tacit expectations of the field and could usefully be instituted in other disciplines. Such courses not only teach literacy skills but, again, increase student's metacognitive ability to assess how they might perform differently. In the course of our study, Paul and Georgia began to envision themselves as psychologists, and Terri took the step of becoming a "real" historian by working with primary materials. We are a bit more skeptical of simply labeling courses "writing-intensive," unless these courses are carefully constructed. Course syllabi may emphasize writing, as for example in the freshman seminar program on our campus, and, yet, student portfolios indicate a wide variety in the kinds and amount of writing actually produced and the kind of instruction and feedback students are given to support this writing.

The upper-level course requirement would replace a second semester of composition at the first-year level. Although our study students included in their portfolios papers from their second composition course and pointed out learning more about research, style, and general essay structure, it is clear that the next major transitions in their development as writers took place as they struggled to integrate the content knowledge, concepts, and research and writing

conventions in their major disciplines. This is the "teachable moment" in which to intervene with a second writing course for this
population of students, a second "space" in the curriculum to focus
on academic literacy.

Assessing Writing Proficiency and Development

Comparing students to each other across academic programs is difficult because, although we might standardize the measuring in-
strument, we can't standardize the students' experience; the development of Sarah's literacy doesn't look the same as Carolyn's,
Kristen's, or Andrea's. The classic "pre-" and "post-" measure of
writing improvement is to take a writing sample before "treatment,"
take a writing sample after "treatment," mix them together and see
whether the "post-'s" get higher scores than the "pre-'s." We chose
not to include this kind of generic, timed writing in our study as not
representative of how students actually negotiate more complex literacy tasks.

But what is the outcome of four years of development? Parents,
administrators, future employers, students themselves, and other
stakeholders are likely to grow weary of complicated explanations
and want to know simply whether students actually improve as
writers as a result of their college experience. The short answer is
that portfolios collected in our study do support the conclusion that
the students did develop new and more complex forms of literacy
over their four years of college. However, a more complicated answer would reflect the cultural/environmental perspective on development that I have argued for throughout this study.

That perspective, elaborated in the work of the developmental
psychologists discussed in this book, maintains that "proficiency"
must be seen in relationship to the specific tasks engaged in by the
learner. Cole (1996) reinforces the point that the cultural perspective takes as "an appropriate unit of analysis . . . a cultural practice,
or activity system, which serves as the proximal environment of
developmental change" (p. 179). The specific cultural practices associated with writing in the university are diverse and complex.

Through multiple interactions with teachers, peers, and texts, students internalize a language and strategies for approaching new reading and writing tasks.

From this perspective, one important measure of students' growth was their increasing metacognitive awareness, their growing ability over four years to describe the methods and conventions of their own disciplines and to point out examples in their portfolios of how they had been able to change their writing to meet these disciplinary expectations. They became better able to assess their own proficiency and target areas where they were still struggling and could continue to improve. The act of assembling a portfolio and reflecting on it during our study helped to promote this kind of growth, as students compared their earlier work to later projects.

Often, students did not identify their growing proficiency as "improvement" in "writing," which many continued to equate with matters of style and grammar taught in English classes. Instead, students focused on their ability to complete challenging literacy tasks they could not have accomplished as first-year students—to read and analyze specialized texts, to conduct research and report on it, and to produce texts, like legal briefs or public relations campaigns, that are intended to do work in the "real" world.

The students' self-reports were supported by evidence in their portfolios, especially the work they selected for their digital portfolios as representative of significant learning. In general, this work had already been judged to be successful by professors in the students' major disciplines. Professors' comments and grades reflected their evaluation that students were proficient enough to successfully complete increasingly more complex tasks in increasingly more difficult courses. By this measure, our study students were quite successful. 14 (70%) of our group of 20 graduated with a GPA above 3.0, 5 (25%) had a GPA above 2.5, and only 1 (5%) was close to a straight "C" average, graduating with a 2.27 in accounting. All of the students included in their digital portfolios at least some "A" and "B" papers written during their college careers.

Oddly enough, although grades are a powerful force in the institutional lives of students, determining their success or failure in gaining academic credentials, grades often are not credited by the institution itself as legitimate markers of proficiency in basic literacy. Timed writing-proficiency tests or standardized portfolios are common ways of attempting to assess performance outside of individual courses, suggesting that institutions are worried about grade inflation or lack of standards and have little faith that their academic programs provide sufficiently rigorous literacy instruction. However, these generic assessments are unlikely to capture the "novel forms and functions" that Cole (1996) notes are the hallmarks of development, unless the assessment is embedded in a specific program with clear goals for literacy that can be articulated by faculty, students, and other stakeholders. Otherwise, a single test can produce only the most reductive measure of how students actually negotiate the complex and messy literacy tasks of their major disciplines.

If professors give grades indicating that students are literate enough to function in their classes, why should a single test function as a gatekeeper? Such tests must necessarily ask students to write a generic essay that could be produced by any student in any major. While these generic essays are similar to texts produced in English composition and some other general education courses, this kind of timed writing on demand is more decontextualized. It plays again to the fantasy that we can produce students who can write on any topic, at any time. Certainly, such tests can accomplish a crude sorting of students based on their ability to produce this kind of essay. However, a test requiring a generic essay ignores the very different kinds of practice in reading, research, and writing that students experience in different courses. For the amount of effort that must be invested in mass testing and grading student essays, there seems to be little payoff in terms of what can be learned about student literacy. And there is a negative payoff for students who are using literacy strategically to accomplish goals set in their classes but must backtrack to learn how to pass the test.

Writing assessment portfolios include more extended samples of student work but are again difficult to standardize across the curriculum. For this study, we chose to collect naturally-occurring examples of student literacy because we were interested in how literacy develops in the day-to-day classroom experience of students. These naturally-occurring samples of writing differ greatly in length, form, style, assumptions about research and evidence, and other conventions. It is possible, of course, to establish a standardized portfolio-assessment program, asking students to submit roughly comparable types of papers and developing generic rubrics for evaluation. Readers can be trained to make gross distinctions of unacceptable, satisfactory, and excellent on generic traits like complexity, organization, development, sentence structure, and usage.

Ideally, however, portfolio assessments are likely to work best within specific programs that have clearly defined goals and a strong sense of how students will acquire the skills being measured. For example, based on what we have learned from our longitudinal study, we are beginning such a portfolio assessment of undergraduate English majors preparing for teaching credentials. As part of a statewide effort, we redefined our goals for prospective teachers, redesigned our curriculum to include a required advanced writing course, and developed assessment rubrics that correspond to our goals. Students are developing digital portfolios that they can use when they apply for teaching positions. This kind of assessment benefits from looking outside of the program as well as within the discipline's courses. We can compare our standards to other credential programs in the state, and importantly, we have asked outstanding classroom teachers who supervise student teachers to let us know the strengths and weaknesses of candidates we send out in the field. For students, working to develop the literacy needed to be an effective teacher seems a more worthwhile goal than simply developing the literacy necessary to pass a test. Comparing work from different courses in the portfolios gives faculty and students a broader view of students' development over time and shows how that development is shaped both by course work and by "hands-on" experiences, like participation in K–12 classrooms.

Following 20 different students over 4 years teaches that there is no one-size-fits-all model of proficiency. As Cole (1996) points out in the quote at the beginning of this chapter, because development leads to the production of novel forms, it cannot be explained in terms of strict cause-effect relationships. Instead, to return to Bronfenbrenner's (1979) more complicated definition, "development is defined as the person's evolving conception of the ecological environment, and his relation to it, as well as the person's growing capacity to discover, sustain, or alter its properties" (p. 4). This development occurs both by accident and by design through the agency of those persons who interact and help "coconstruct" their environments. Cole emphasizes, "mind emerges in the joint mediated activity of people" (p. 104). Although young adults interact in many different, interlocking environments, the school plays a special role. Ideally, this learning subcommunity "models ways of doing or knowing, provides opportunities for emulation, offers running commentary, provides 'scaffolding' for novices, and even provides a good context for teaching deliberately," reflecting to the young adult "how well she is going about her job and how her approach can be improved" (Bruner, 1996, p. 21). The most effective learning subcommunities involve students in assessing their own literacy development, while providing the scaffolding necessary to develop new skills.

Recommendations for Instruction

How can learning communities best provide the scaffolding to support learners in their development from novice college writers to more mature adults able to take on complex problems requiring advanced abilities to communicate? Though there are no universal solutions, this study suggests several recommendations for instruction that will be useful for composition specialists responsible for first-year programs and also for faculty across the disciplines. These recommendations are guided by the perspectives developed in this study. In revising instruction methods, we need to think about the student's environment from the student's perspective.

1. Rethink student work as "literacy tasks" and not "writing assignments." Focus on writing "differently," not just "better."

To think developmentally means taking a broader view of student "writing." When professors assign "writing" and students are unsuccessful, professors may assume that students don't know "how to write." In fact, the kind of critical literacy required in college needs to be more broadly defined to include the ability to understand and use different methods of inquiry, sources of information (including other people and nonprint media), ways of working (including collaboration), forms of technology, and genres or types of reading and writing. It is helpful to think through all of the things a student must know and be able to do to complete an assigned task. What makes a successful response? When we compare the work of successful and unsuccessful students, what does the successful student know and do that is missing from the work of less successful students? The effective response may just look better with correct sentence structure and spelling, but unless the assignment is very simple, it will probably do much more. The students in our study were not bothered much by problems of punctuation or spelling, and yet they struggled with new tasks—how to approach a problem, how to find information, how to read difficult material, how to write in an appropriate academic style, and, especially, how to apply all of the new concepts and content knowledge they were rapidly acquiring. In addition, they needed to develop writing processes for actually producing coherent texts during the time, which was never enough, allotted for sometimes many different writing projects. The papers in the students' final portfolios indicated that, in varying degrees, they brought from high school the literacy skills to begin these tasks but that they needed to transform their "normal" ways of reading, writing, and thinking to meet the expectations of a new environment.

2. Conduct an audit of writing within academic majors or other specific programs and fill in gaps in literacy instruction.

Examining student development over time, where will students learn the concepts and skills to meet the literacy demands of their disciplines? English composition is an "introductory," general education course. In our study, most students in English I and II were introduced to some general conventions of academic writing, especially the expectation that writers make assertions and support these with explanations, evidence, analysis, or other appropriate development. Students also learned some basic research skills, especially how to work with written sources, and reported, in some cases, learning, usually through teacher commentary and conferences, ways to improve their writing through revision and editing. But because students encountered so many different literacy tasks in their careers, an emphasis on any one kind of writing in first-year composition was unlikely to carry over into the more specific genres of writing in students' particular academic disciplines. Instead of mastering one particular style of writing, students needed to develop flexibility as writers, especially the ability to analyze different rhetorical situations and adapt writing strategies accordingly. First-year composition was a space in the curriculum where students could practice new ways of writing without the additional burden of learning, at the same time, extensive content knowledge in an academic discipline. Students had the opportunity or were forced, depending on their point of view, to experiment with personal style and voice and to examine the ways in which language shapes our views of the world and ourselves.

But even for these relatively experienced writers working in small classes in pleasant surroundings, this one or two semester introduction to writing did not transform them into those fantasy students who could write anywhere, anytime, on any topic. We need to examine more closely how students' literacy education will continue beyond their first year. Major disciplines and programs need to consider, again, not just "writing," but what kinds of critical literacy they want students to develop. The model, in many courses, of two or three tests and a paper at the end of the semester does not give most students sufficient practice and feedback to become truly proficient. Again, it is helpful to collect portfolios of student work, in this case, across different courses within the major and compare the work of successful and less successful students. While many departments collect class syllabi and assignments, portfolios provide a clearer picture of student development. What teachers ask for in assignments and what students actually write are often not the same. For example, when we arranged for teachers to compare portfolios across sections in our composition program, we discovered that although course guidelines were similar, the amount and kinds of writing produced in different classes were not the same. Comparing portfolios led us to develop greater consensus about how much writing students should complete in a semester and what kinds of writing should be emphasized.

In our longitudinal study, the amount of student writing was often uneven across semesters with much writing in some periods and none in others. This may be appropriate with some courses building a broad base of knowledge and others asking for application and in-depth thinking; however, students need to develop both ways of knowing throughout their college experience. In courses like research methods, students can focus directly on what counts as evidence in their field and how that evidence is generally presented. Writing-intensive courses should not merely assign more writing but need to provide direct instruction and practice in using sources, reporting data, applying concepts, constructing arguments, and writing in genres appropriate to the discipline.

3. Redesign the literacy environment to provide more options, in addition to those found in the academic majors, where students study material in-depth and negotiate complex literacy tasks over a sequence of courses.

This recommendation comes with some reservations. There is always a tension between breadth and depth in undergraduate education. Some students in our study, especially those undecided about a major, valued the variety of different courses in general education. Depth of knowledge was developed through courses offered within disciplinary majors. In addition, study students developed additional depth in disciplinary minors or in their own unofficial concentrations, where they combined required general education courses and electives to follow special interests in art, African American studies, foreign language, and other subjects.

However, environment matters, so if we want to change development, we need to restructure the environment. Students do best what they do most. The Great Books sequence of four courses at

Pepperdine, discussed in chapter 3, provides an example of this kind of in-depth learning. In addition to developing concepts and content knowledge, students over two years were explicitly taught a particular way of reading, discussing, writing, and critical thinking. While one might argue over what students should read and what kinds of writing, reading, and thinking skills they should be learning, the Great Books sequence does illustrate that complex literacy skills develop best with repeated practice over time and that students develop the particular types of critical literacy that they practice. Simply requiring several courses in a subject does not necessarily develop this sort of critical literacy. For example, students at Pepperdine are required to take three religion courses. While these do an admirable job of teaching about religion, they are designed for a broad range of students and are not structured to provide consistent practice in ways of writing critically about religious issues.

The Great Books sequence is able to create a rich literacy environment with small classes; self-selected, committed students and teachers; an emphasis on reading challenging primary texts; a uniform curriculum and method focused on critical thinking; and the leisure to consider concepts and content in-depth over four semesters. To what extent could this sequence be replicated with subjects of interest to other groups of students—the arts, political issues, science and ecology, ethnic studies? At Pepperdine, faculty have experimented with collaboration between composition courses and more content-based courses, as a way of carving out a little more time in the general education curriculum for students to read, write, discuss, and think deeply about issues. Coordinating such collaborations can be a bureaucratic nightmare and requires a commitment from both students and teachers. It is difficult to maintain the balance between focusing on content and focusing on students' own literacy development. Without this balance, coordinated course sequences can become merely extensions to majors that are always seeking to expand their required units. This pressure to train students only as specialists and future workers neglects their potential to act in other important roles, especially as broadly educated citizens. Course sequences on the model of the Great Books seminars can emphasize diverse ways of knowing and not simply add to the student's stockpile of information. Structurally, such sequences seem easiest to initiate and maintain if they are relatively small, self-selected by both teachers and students, and not mass produced with a "one-size-fits-all" curriculum. These sequences may exist in conjunction with more broad survey courses, again giving students a balance between knowing about subject matter and knowing how to analyze and produce knowledge themselves as critically literate persons.

To some extent, however, rich literacy environments, like the well-funded Great Books program, may remain a luxury available primarily to already successful students in schools seeking to court well-off parents and donors. Creating such environments is expensive, and when programs are mandated without adequate funding, they may simply reshuffle configurations of students and teachers, often part-timers and graduate students, without really changing the learning environment. And for all their luxury, even the best-designed programs will still not fulfill the fantasy that students will learn to read, write, speak, and think, once and for always. In the Great Books sequence or any other we might initiate, students will learn a particular way of approaching texts and ideas, perhaps valuable, but, nonetheless, a way that must be rethought and relearned when they move into new contexts.

4. Develop projects and assignments that will challenge all students even if students' finished products are less than perfect. Take seriously students' questions about "what the professor wants" and provide clearly explained assignments, guidelines for performance, models, specific feedback, and opportunities for self-assessment and improvement.

Student work looks more finished and competent when students have less challenging assignments that they already know how to do. Students who were generally successful in high school can be successful with little effort on relatively simple literacy tasks. However, these assignments do not move students to develop new literacy skills. Students will work toward the level of critical literacy called for in assignments and tests. On challenging tasks, students' initial performance may be unsatisfactory, and this less than successful work can be frustrating to both students and professors. But students can improve with feedback, self-assessment, and opportunities to revise their initial efforts or apply new skills in subsequent assignments. Students' progress can be slow, and we need to be able to tolerate less than perfect trial runs. Interestingly, students did not pick only their best work for their digital portfolios. They also included writing that was far from perfect but that illustrated significant turning points in their learning.

Writing performance and student learning are not identical. For example, although Andrea's performance as a writer remained uneven over her four-year college career, she clearly demonstrated new concepts, content knowledge, and ways of writing in response to the challenging assignments in her major. Some professors actually say they do not assign writing because students do not know "how to write." Whose sensibilities are they protecting? It may be romantic to be so in love with language that you cannot bear to see it misused by mere students; however, this does not make for good teaching.

As Terri said, "Professors assume that you know. Maybe everybody else knows but I didn't know." From the students' perspective, the only universal truth about college writing is that if you want to be successful, you have to give professors what they want. The least professors can do is make these expectations clear. Some professors say that all they want is "good writing" or that they want students to be original. In fact, I can think of one professor in our study who did encourage students to write very free-ranging essays and rewarded them for doing so. However, most professors have hidden or not-so-hidden agendas. Professors may think of explaining and modeling what is expected in literacy tasks as hand holding or remedial work. In fact, this support helps students bridge the gap between what they can already do and the new tasks they face in college.

The strategies for this kind of teaching are familiar from writing-across-the-curriculum workshops and guidebooks. (See, for example,

Bean (1996) *Engaging Ideas: A Professor's Guide To Integrating Writing, Critical Thinking, and Active Learning in the Classroom.*) I will summarize a few of the most common suggestions supported by our longitudinal study. Students appreciate assignments given in writing with specific guidelines for how the work will be evaluated. The assignment sheet may include a timeline of steps students will need to take to complete the project. Students respond to what they perceive as important to the professor, especially as these concerns are reflected in grading. If certain editing errors, like the difference between "its" and "it's" or the fact that commas at the end of a quote go *inside* the quotation marks, drive the professor crazy, preparing an editing check-sheet of key items and warning of dire penalties for violations can alert students to pay careful attention to such matters. Specific guidelines work better than simply exhorting students to write well.

In addition to guidelines, however, students need to see examples of successful and unsuccessful work within their disciplines. While students can learn some disciplinary conventions from reading professional articles, examples of student work illustrate the kinds of writing they themselves can reasonably be expected to produce. Most important are examples showing students how one makes assertions *and* supports them in the discipline or how one reports data and analyzes them. This balance between reporting information and constructing an argument or analysis is the most difficult for students to maintain. When students are given several sample student papers to evaluate, they themselves can usually identify the strategies used by more successful writers.

Providing feedback on student work is time consuming, but five well-chosen comments may be as effective as fifty-five very specific marks. How students take up professor comments depends on the context in which they are made. Professors in our study created a context for commentary in a variety of ways—by asking students to evaluate their own work with check-sheets or written self-assessments, by involving students in critiquing each other's work, by meeting with students in individual conferences. Ideally, this commentary occurred before the last week of the semester, so students had opportunities to revise their work or to apply what they had learned on subsequent assignments.

Professors may feel that time spent on literacy takes away from the important concepts and content knowledge they need to teach in their disciplines. However, learning how to read, research, and write has to be part of what it means to "know" a particular field. Professors have so much tacit experience in this way of knowing that it takes a conscious effort to model for students how this critical literacy works.

5. Provide scaffolding to support development by directly teaching discipline specific research and writing skills, using grading strategically to reward improvement, scheduling interim deadlines for longer projects, and requiring classroom workshops, study groups, and teacher conferences. Create more opportunities for "hands-on" learning which may include guest speakers, field trips, projects, service learning, internships, and other connections between the classroom and communities outside the classroom.

As students acquire content knowledge in their academic disciplines, they also become more proficient in reading and writing the language of the discipline. However, this process is clearly accelerated when teachers focus specifically on the research skills and writing genres they expect students to employ. After completing the research-methods course in psychology which included intensive practice in writing, Paul and Georgia were able to explain more clearly disciplinary conventions and point out how they had changed their own work to write in a more professional way. Similarly, being guided through a major project, using primary resources, in an introductory history research-methods course helped Terri develop a deeper understanding of ways of reading and writing in her field.

However, despite these experiences, students often do not demonstrate the full range of their literacy skills. In most cases, the papers they turn in to professors are essentially first drafts. While students may revise as they write and leave a little time for a quick edit, their papers are usually produced close to final deadlines. This seems to work for students who often get "B's" and, not infrequently, "A's" on these drafts. This may be a perfectly acceptable writing process. There is no intrinsic value in revision for revision's sake. We are all strategic about literacy and often do not revise first drafts of texts, like letters or routine memos, that can satisfy an audience the first time around. However, if professors are dissatisfied with student writing, they may try to intervene in students' usual last-minute, one-draft approach to writing. Again, I don't want to over-emphasize the importance of grades, but our study showed that at Pepperdine, if not at other universities, students are very grade conscious and interpret the grade on a paper as the strongest signal of how well they are doing. A "C" is not an acceptable grade for most students in our college. Certainly, students are also motivated by their personal interests, course content, and rapport with the professor, but as busy people, they are more likely to take part in re-quired, *graded* class activities rather than in optional opportunities for improvement. However, just grading harder doesn't necessarily motivate students to improve. In Terri's case, for example, she took her "C" grades in English and looked around for a different major. "Tearing apart" student papers only seemed to work when students knew they could ultimately benefit from this process. Susanna and Kristen improved in science by applying on subsequent lab reports what they learned from the extensive criticism of their first at-tempts.

How students are graded can influence their writing processes. When grades are focused entirely on a final written product, stu-dents may underestimate the literacy tasks they are being asked to complete. They may see the task as simply "writing up," as quickly as possible, the information most readily available. On the other hand, dividing the points for a project into separate grades for an initial research report, a preliminary draft, and a revision, for example, signals to students that the professor takes seriously each step in the process. Requiring study groups, writing workshops, or individual conferences ensures that all students, not just the best and most motivated, take advantage of different ways of learning.

Journals, reading responses, and other informal writing not only promote learning but also serve as interim steps to prepare for major exams and projects. However, students are likely to view these activities as busywork, unless they are closely related to the goals of the course and pay off in terms of improvement in their learning and course grade.

Students in our study often selected "hands-on" experiences as most significant to their learning. Those who had studied in international programs especially contrasted the benefits of learning language, history, literature, art, politics, and other subjects while living in a foreign country with their experience of learning primarily in the classroom. Closer to home, students commended projects and internships that took them into museums, businesses, churches, community organizations, and other sites where they could connect their classroom learning to an adult world outside of school. "Translation/critical literacy" as defined by Miles Myers (1996) requires that adults not only be able to decode and analyze texts but flexibly shift language strategies as appropriate to different problems, modes of communication, sign-systems, and discourse communities. School, alone, does not provide enough variety of environments for students to practice different literacy strategies nor demonstrate to students why they would want to learn different ways of knowing.

This "hands-on" learning can be time consuming to organize. However, the connection to the world off-campus can be as simple as inviting a guest speaker to class, requiring students to visit a museum and write a brief report, or including an interview with a local "expert" as part of a research project. When such activities are required, not optional, it also means an extra time investment for students. However, all students, not just the best and brightest, can benefit from observations, internships, and other off-campus experiences.

6. Reconsider with students, colleagues, and other professionals in your discipline whether "what the professor wants" is, in fact, what the discipline needs or should want. Encourage at least some experiments with writing in different forms for different audiences,

writing that resists or reinterprets disciplinary conventions, writing that explores students' values and ethics as related to discipline-specific issues.

As I discussed in chapter 4, students frequently resisted the expectations of their individual professors, but our study students never seriously questioned discipline-specific conventions and rarely stepped intentionally outside the boundaries of what an assignment required. Most assignments in the disciplines were based on conventional academic or professional writing in the field—historical studies, literary criticism, researched reports, case studies, lab reports, public relations projects, et cetera. These genres of writing were appropriate in promoting student learning, in encouraging students' development as writers, and in preparing them for future studies or careers. However, disciplinary studies and careers do change over time, knowledge is coconstructed in language and can be reconstructed to achieve new goals. In addition to predictable disciplinary forms, models of writing introduced to students might demonstrate some diversity—work from serious, general magazines; short professional memos; cutting-edge scholarly work; popular writing in newspapers and trade books; documentaries, debates, newscasts. Otherwise, as students get comfortable with the conventions of their field, they may become uncomfortable with innovation. As Kristen wrote after three years as a science major, "I'm so used to being a straightforward writer that I'm rusty on my creativity."

This does not mean that students need to add what Andrea called "frilly stuff" to all their writing. However, students might try transforming knowledge by explaining what they know to a nonspecialist audience. They might analyze what is gained and lost when the same information is cast in different genres, and they might prepare for more active roles as citizens by applying what they know in writing editorials, reviews, letters, and brochures. They may use current technology to develop web sites or graphic displays. Formal and conventional pieces of writing might be accompanied by short, informal letters or journals explaining how the student developed her research and writing, the problems she had along the way, and the opinions or insights that did not seem to fit in the final, formal draft. At least some writing should ask students to reflect on the values and ethics of the work they do as students and the careers they plan to pursue.

In a recent writing-across-the-curriculum workshop at Pepperdine, faculty actually enjoyed exchanging "alternative" writing assignments prompted by suggestions in Bean's (1996) *Engaging Ideas*. Faculty later enjoyed reading the "creative" responses written by their students. For example, writers in a religion course imagined encountering the prophet Amos as a street preacher in Santa Monica and tried to interpret his social justice message for an affluent contemporary audience; sports medicine students applied the characteristics of peak performance and "flow" to describe examples of these states in their own experience; and psychology students developed their own questions based on chapters they had read, explaining not the answers to the questions but why the questions themselves were significant. These "low stakes" assignments, counting about the same as a quiz grade, were rather quickly evaluated by faculty and provided surprising insights into what students did or did not understand about their topics. These assignments asked students to apply concepts in different contexts, raise their own questions, and write in varying formats.

Thinking Longitudinally

Perhaps, my account of students' literacy development at Pepperdine sounds overly optimistic in light of alarmist claims that our current generation of students can barely read and write. Pepperdine students are in many ways privileged when compared with some of their peers at other postsecondary institutions. They are more likely to have small classes, close contact with professors, and opportunities for foreign study and internships. Most live on campus, at least during their first year, in a very beautiful physical setting. They enjoy well-equipped and well-maintained classrooms. For many, this pleasant setting echoes the lifestyles they have been accustomed to at home and reassures them that this lifestyle will continue as they move into careers. The physical structure of educational settings subtly tells students what they are worth and is part of the way schools sort students for future status. Pepperdine tells students they are worth at least $24,000 a year. This pleasant environment can promote complacency and a sense of entitlement. Students may feel life is good for them and wonder why others in society are complaining.

It would be a mistake, however, to view our students as homogeneous. Although this study has focused on the participants' roles as "students," these young adults are much more, and each has a different family background and educational history. Because of the small size of our sample and even though there were more women than men, I chose not to single out individual students as representative of the experiences of their gender, race, or class. But, clearly, not all students felt at home in this affluent setting. Andrea, as an African American student, had to search through the curriculum to find the few courses that fulfilled her interest in African American studies. Terri was also disappointed by the lack of diversity among students and courses. In addition, Terri, like several other students in our study, had to maintain a complicated financial-aid package, worked to earn additional money, and still left college with a substantial burden of loans.

And students in our study rarely discussed with me the darker side of their student experience. I know from my own courses that plagiarism sometimes masks students' inability to complete literacy tasks, but this subject was not brought up by students in our study, and I failed to probe the topic. More seriously, I know that one of our least successful study students certainly suffered from incapacitating depressions. But, again, this was not an area she wished to discuss with me in-depth. Students' performances do not always reflect their competence or their potential. As young adults, students struggle with family problems, relationships, physical and mental health issues, and the choices they must make about their futures.

Nonetheless, perhaps students at Pepperdine do not reflect the general state of literacy among college students in California and across the country. In order to achieve equity in our society, we must focus much of our attention on our least successful students, those underserved by inadequate schools. In California, the decline in funding for education, due to property tax reform and state budget cuts, condemned many students to ill-equipped classrooms with untrained and inadequately trained teachers. Much of our effort must be addressed to eliminating the inequities between our best public and private schools and those that are not adequately educating children. And yet, we cannot label whole groups of students as necessarily "underprepared" for college. Over the past twenty years, I have worked with the California Writing Project, and I have seen talented, dedicated teachers and students working on remarkable literacy projects in K–12 schools all across the state, including those schools with the fewest economic resources. Students who want to continue their educations, despite economic hardships, deserve access to postsecondary institutions and opportunities to develop advanced literacy skills. Students do reach community colleges and universities ready to do college-level work or, at the very least, ready to *begin* learning to do college-level work.

Although we need to continue to focus attention on those students who will need the most support to negotiate the complex literacy tasks required in college, what happens to those students who consider themselves "good writers," or at least adequately prepared for writing in college, and who fill many of the seats in our classrooms? I hope I have shown that they are worthy of study. They will likely fulfill a variety of roles in our society as future teachers, journalists, lawyers, mid-level managers and leaders in business, government, and the professions. Even though they were generally successful in high school, they begin again with new roles and new challenges in college. Throughout the study, I have been impressed by the growth of their knowledge and their ability to read, write, and think in new and more complex ways. They have been inspired and supported by many of their teachers. I have also been disappointed by lost opportunities and times when students have not been challenged or have been frustrated by school and, some-times, personal circumstances in their efforts to grow.

I want to end with a quote from Cynthia Ozick's (1983) novel, *The Cannibal Galaxy*. Hester Lilt, a philosopher, writer, and the mother of a child thought to be "slow," is giving a talk on the topic, "An Interpretation of Pedagogy." She comments on the story of four rabbis viewing the ruins of their sacred temple. Three of the rabbis weep, but the fourth laughs. He explains that he sees the scene of destruction as a good sign, because according to prophecy, the temple had to be destroyed before it could be rebuilt.

> "And *that*," says Hester Lilt in her commentary, "is peda-gogy. To predict not from the first text, but from the sec-ond. Not from the earliest evidence, but from the latest. To laugh out loud in that very interval which to every rea-sonable judgement looks to be the most inappropriate— when the first is accomplished and future repair is most chimerical. To expect, to welcome exactly that which ap-pears most unpredictable. To await the surprise which, when it comes, turns out to be not a surprise after all, but a natural path." (p. 68)

I began this study by referring to some of the doubts that aca-demics in composition studies currently express about the work they have traditionally undertaken. These doubts raise several ques-tions: What is the role of first-year composition? How do writ-ing abilities develop across the curriculum? What can we learn from ongoing assessments? Ozick, speaking in the voice of Hester Lilt, reminds us to look at the big picture, to think longitudinally. Literacy development in schools is not a "natural path." It is shaped by the environment of schools—coconstructed by teachers, stu-dents, and other stakeholders. And, yet, it does occur in ways that are not entirely predictable. Composition specialists can be advo-cates for students, tracing how this development occurs, encourag-ing faculty and students to expect development which, at times, may seem chimerical, and suggesting ways to fill the gaps between the first college writing and the last. Students, as they rehearse new roles, struggle to make these connections. Our continuing research and debates about first-year composition need to situate this course at the students' transition to college and also within the larger picture of students' literacy development. Work in writing-across-the-curriculum programs is likely to continue to be slow, messy, and underfunded, as literacy remains a tacit, not focal, element in most academic disciplines. And yet, this is where students develop their complex literacy and where they need the most support. Assessment, a current darling of administrators and accrediting agencies, can actually open a window on development, if assessments are embedded in and reflect the real literacy projects students undertake during their college experience. Composition specialists are unlikely to restructure the global environment of higher education, but with a longitudinal perspective, we can act locally to support literacy development and expect unpredictable surprises along the way.

Appendix A

A.1: Methods and Materials

This study began as part of the CD–ROM Portfolio Assessment Project, a broad effort to assess learning in general education courses at Seaver College, the undergraduate school of Pepperdine University. As the project evolved, it became possible to store materials on web pages as well as to create CD–ROM's, and current assessment projects using portfolios continue under a new title, the Digital Portfolio Assessment Project (DPAP). Articles on assessment at Pepperdine and links to assessment sites at other institutions and organizations are accessible at http://assess.pepperdine.edu. Most of the student portfolios analyzed in this study are also available at our web site. Several students in the study did complete interviews and choose materials for a final portfolio, but they did so after the deadlines, which technical staff had established, to scan and digitize their work. Students' digital portfolios are password protected but academic researchers can request a password by contacting our director of assessment through our web site.

The Assessment Office web site can also be accessed by going to the Pepperdine University home page at http://www.pepperdine.edu. Point to schools and click on Seaver College. From the quick search directory on the Seaver College home page, click on assessment office.

Student self-assessment forms and interview questions used in this study are on the following pages of Appendix A.

A.2: CD–ROM Portfolio Assessment
School Year _____

Student ID# _____

Please answer the following questions, as they relate to your portfolio of work completed during the past school year.

1. Give examples of 1 or 2 pieces of work (assignments, projects, tests, et cetera) that you think represent significant learning during this year. Why is this work especially important?

2. What are 1 or 2 specific things that you did that helped you learn from this work?

3. What are 1 or 2 specific things that your instructor did that helped you learn from this work?

4. Give 1 or 2 examples of work from this year that you think were less successful, where you did not learn as much. How do they demonstrate less successful learning?

5. What are 1 or 2 things that you did that hindered you or interfered with your learning on this assignment, project, test, et cetera?

6. What are 1 or 2 specific things your instructor did that hindered or interfered with your learning on this work?

7. During the summer, faculty researchers will be reviewing student portfolios. What can they find out about student learning by looking at your portfolio? Please give one or two examples of things you would like them to notice about your work.

8. How well does your portfolio capture your learning during this year? Give one or two examples of important

learning experiences that are not represented in your portfolio.

9. What are the benefits students might experience from participating in the CD–ROM Portfolio Project?

10. How could the project be improved for next year?

11. Will you participate in the project for another year? Explain why or why not.

A.3: CD–ROM Student Portfolio Project

Interview Questions: Yearly Interview

We all experience change in various areas of our academic, social, emotional, and spiritual life from year to year. The purpose of this interview session is to allow you to respond reflectively about the changes that you have experienced during the last year.

Please look over the following list and indicate if you feel you have changed in any of these categories since last year. Mark each response with a 0—no change, 1—slight change, 2—some change, or 3—significant change.

Question	Response
1. Reason for being in college	_____
2. Interest in your major	_____
3. Involvement in service/volunteer work	_____
4. Desire to learn	_____
5. Interest/involvement with other cultures	_____
6. Personal, ethical, and moral values	_____
7. Communication skills	_____
8. Mathematical and quantitative skills	_____
9. Desire to get a high-paying job	_____
10. Desire to develop a meaningful worldview	_____
11. Attitude toward general education courses	_____
12. Interest in living/working overseas	_____
13. Seeing relationships between different courses	_____

14. Connecting experiences in and out of
    the classroom   _____
15. Critical thinking skills   _____

A.4: CD–ROM Portfolio Project

Writing Interview: Senior Year

1. What is your major now? Have you changed majors?
   Why? What were your previous major(s)? What is
   your career goal?

2. (Ask student to review areas of change.) In which areas listed on our yearly interview questionnaire have
   you changed most since your freshman year? Explain.

3. Focusing on writing, has your writing changed over
   the years you have been in college? Explain.

4. What experiences in college, either positive or negative, have been most important to your writing?

5. Have classes or teachers helped you with your writing? How?

6. What have you yourself done that has had an impact
   on your writing?
   What difficulties have you had, if any?
   What writing strategies have you developed?
   How would you evaluate your own skill as a writer at
   this point?
   How important is writing in your academic life and in
   your future career?

7. What else could your teachers have done or could you
   have done yourself that might have helped you be a
   better writer?

8. Have experiences outside of the classroom been

important to your writing? Explain. Could you give me a sample of that writing?

9. Could we review some samples of writing from your portfolio?
   For each year, would you choose at least one sample of work that you think is representative of your development at that time?
   For each piece, please answer the following questions: How is this piece representative or typical of your writing during your ____ year?
   Tell me about this assignment. What can we learn about you and your development by looking at this piece?
   For pieces written after the first year, please answer the following questions: Does this show a change in your writing? How? Explain.

10. Can I check on some background information? What is your age now? Where are you from? Where did you go to high school? What are your parents' occupations?

Appendix B
The Students

Name	Major (Minor)	Univ. Cum. GPA	H.S. GPA	SAT Math	SAT Verbal	Ethnicity
Randall	Biology	3.23	3.42	570	580	W
Kristen	Sports Medicine	2.96	3.55	520	590	W
Susanna	Sports Medicine	3.84	4.00	28 ACT	31 ACT	W
George	Sports Med./Bus.Admin.	3.29	3.31	420	590	W
Stephen	Psychology (Religion)	3.41	3.50	31 ACT	23 ACT	W
Paul	Psychology	3.18	3.50	580	650	W
Georgia	Psychology	2.69	2.96	400	430	W
Andrea	Political Science	3.05	3.69	470	530	AA
Terri	History	2.68	3.36	450	610	AA
Sarah	English (Philosophy)	3.71	4.00	510	620	W
Elizabeth	English	2.56	3.22	480	410	W
Natalie	Public Relations (Music)	3.10	3.50	540	480	W
Carolyn	Public Relations	3.67	3.58	500	560	W
Vanessa	Journalism (Spanish)	3.14	2.74	410	470	H
Leslie	Marketing/Ad	3.88	4.00	620	520	W
Deborah	Telecommunications (Art)	3.63	3.80	620	620	W
Jeanette	Accounting	2.27	3.16	450	480	W
Allison	Accounting	3.25	3.88	570	590	W
Julia	Bus. Admin.	3.33	3.80	620	610	W
Bhakti	Bus. Admin.	2.69	3.52	480	480	A

References

Adler-Kassner, L. (2000). Structure and possibility: New scholarship about students-called-basic-writers. *College English, 63* (2), 229–243.

Adler-Kassner, L., Crooks, R., & Watters, A. (Eds.). (1997). *Writing the community: Concepts and models for service-learning in composition.* Washington, D.C.: American Association of Higher Education.

Alberti, J. (2001). Returning to class: Creating opportunity for multicultural reform at majority second-tier schools. *College English, 63* (5), 561–584.

Allison, L., Bryant, L., & Hourigan, M. (Eds.). (1997). *Grading in the post-process classroom: From theory to practice.* Portsmouth, NH: Boynton/Cook.

Anderson, W., Best, C., Black, A., Hurst, J., Miller, B., & Miller, S. (1990). Cross-curricular underlife: A collaborative report on ways with academic words. *College Composition and Communication, 41* (1), 11–36.

Applebee, A. (1984). *Contexts for learning to write: Studies of secondary school instruction.* Norwood, NJ: Ablex.

Bartholomae, D. (1985). Inventing the university. In M. Rose (Ed.), *When a writer can't write: Studies in writer's block and other composing problems* (pp. 134–165). New York: Guilford.

Bean, J. (1996). *Engaging ideas: A professor's guide to integrating writing, critical thinking, and active learning in the classroom.* San Francisco: Jossey-Bass.

Berlin, J. (1992). Poststructuralism, cultural studies, and the composition classroom: Postmodern theory in practice. *Rhetoric Review, 11* (1), 16–33.

Berlin, J. (1996). *Rhetorics, poetics, and cultures: Refiguring college English studies.* Urbana, IL: NCTE.

Bizzell, P. (1992). *Academic discourse and critical consciousness.* Pittsburgh, PA: University of Pittsburgh Press.

Bowles, S. & Gintis, H. (1976). *Schooling in capitalist America: Educational reform and the contradictions of economic life.* New York: Basic Books.

Britton, J., Burgess, T., Martin, N., McLeod, A., & Rosen, H. (1975). *The development of writing abilities (11–18).* London: Macmillan.

Brodkey, L. (1987). *Academic writing as social practice.* Philadelphia: Temple University Press.

Bronfenbrenner, U. (1979). *The ecology of human development: Experiments by nature and design.* Cambridge, MA: Harvard University Press.

Brooke, R. & Hendricks, J. (1989). *Audience expectations and teacher demands.* Carbondale, IL: Southern Illinois University Press.

Brueggemann, B. (1996). Still-life: Representations and silences in the participant-observer role. In P. Mortenson & G. Kirsch (Eds.), *Ethics and Representation in Qualitative Studies of Literacy* (pp. 17–39). Urbana, IL: NCTE.

Bruner, J. (1986). *Actual minds, possible worlds.* Cambridge, MA: Harvard University Press.

Bruner, J. (1996). *The culture of education.* Cambridge, MA: Harvard University Press.

Carroll, L. (1997). Pomo blues: Stories from first-year composition. *College English,* 59 (8), 916–933.

Chiseri-Strater, E. (1991). *Academic literacies: The public and private discourse of university students.* Portsmouth, NH: Boynton/Cook.

Clifford, J. & Schilb, J. (Eds.). (1994). *Writing theory and critical theory.* New York: Modern Language Association.

Cole, M. (1996). *Cultural psychology: The once and future discipline.* Cambridge, MA: Harvard University Press.

Cole, M. & Scribner, S. (1981). *The psychology of literacy.* Cambridge, MA: Harvard University Press.

Connors, R. (1996). The abolition debate in composition: A short history. In L. Bloom, D. Daiker, & E. White (Eds.), *Composition in the twenty-first century: Crisis and change* (pp. 47–63). Carbondale, IL: Southern Illinois University Press.

Cooper, C. & MacDonald, S. (Eds.). (2000). *Writing the world: Reading and writing about issues of the day.* Boston: Bedford/St. Martins.

Cooper, C. & Odell, L. (Eds.). (1998). *Evaluating writing: The role of teachers' knowledge about text, learning, and culture.* Urbana, IL: NCTE.

Cooper, M. (1986). The ecology of writing. *College English,* 48 (4), 364–375.

Cooper, M. (1990). The answers are not in the back of the book: Developing discourse practices in first-year English. In R. Beach & S. Hynds (Eds.), *Developing discourse practices in adolescence and adulthood* (pp. 65–90). Norwood, NJ: Ablex.

Crowley, S. (1991). A personal essay on freshman English. *Pre/Text,* 12, 156–76.

Crowley, S. (1998). *Composition in the university: Historical and polemical essays.* Pittsburgh, PA: University of Pittsburgh Press.

Crowson, R. (1994). Qualitative research methods in higher education. In N. Denzin & Y. Lincoln (Eds.), *Handbook of qualitative research* (pp. 167–208). Newbury Park, CA: Sage.

Denzin, N. & Lincoln, Y. (Eds.). (1994). *Handbook of qualitative research.* Newbury Park, CA: Sage.

Durst, R. (1999). *Collision course: Conflict, negotiation, and learning in college composition.* Urbana, IL: NCTE.

Ehrenreich, B. (1989). *Fear of falling: The inner life of the middle class.* New York: Random House.

Faigley, L. (1992). *Fragments of rationality: Postmodernity and the subject of composition.* Pittsburgh, PA: University of Pittsburgh Press.

Fox, T. (1999). *Defending access: A critique of standards in higher education.* Portsmouth, NH: Boynton/Cook.

Freire, P. (1982). *Pedagogy of the oppressed.* (Myra Bergman Ramos, Trans.). New York: Continuum. (Original work published 1970).

Geisler, C. (1994). *Academic literacy and the nature of expertise: Reading, writing, and knowing in academic philosophy.* Hillsdale, NJ: Erlbaum.

Giroux, H. (1981). *Ideology, culture, and the process of schooling.* Philadelphia: Temple University Press.

Gleason, Barbara. (2000). Evaluating writing programs in real time: The politics of remediation. *College Composition and Communication, 51* (4), 560–588.

Haas, C. (1994). Learning to read biology: One student's rhetorical development in college. *Written Communication, 11* (1), 43–84.

Harkin, P. & Schilb, J. (Eds.). (1991). *Contending with words: Composition and rhetoric in a postmodern age.* New York: Modern Language Association.

Heath, S. (1983). *Ways with words: Language, life, and work in communities and classrooms.* Cambridge, England: Cambridge University Press.

Herrington, A. & Moran, C. (Eds.). (1992). *Writing, teaching, and learning in the disciplines.* New York: Modern Language Association.

Jolliffe, D. (Ed.). (1988). *Advances in writing research, volume two: Writing in academic disciplines.* Norwood, NJ: Ablex.

Krashen, S. (1984). *Writing: Research, theory, applications.* Oxford, England: Pergamon Press.

MacDonald, S. (1994). *Professional academic writing in the humanities and social sciences.* Carbondale, IL: Southern Illinois University Press.

McLaren, P. & Lankshear, C. (1993). Critical literacy and the postmodern turn. In P. McLaren and C. Lankshear (Eds.), *Critical literacy: Politics, praxis, and the postmodern* (pp. 379–419). Albany, NY: State University of New York Press.

Miller, S. (1991). *Textual carnivals: The politics of composition.* Carbondale, IL: Southern Illinois University Press.

Mortensen, P. & Kirsch, G. (1996). *Ethics and representation in qualitative studies of literacy.* Urbana, IL: NCTE.

Myers, M. (1996). *Changing our minds: Negotiating English and literacy.* Urbana, IL: NCTE.

Ozick, C. (1983). *The cannibal galaxy.* New York: Knopf.

Rose, M. (1990). *Lives on the boundary: A moving account of the struggles and achievements of America's educational underclass.* New York: Penguin.

Scardamalia, M. (1981). How children cope with the cognitive demands of writing. In C. H. Frederiksen and J. F. Dominic (Eds.), *Writing: The nature, development, and teaching of written communication.* Vol. 2. *Writing: Process, development, and communication.* Hillsdale, NJ: Erlbaum.

Segal, J., Pare, A., Brent, D., & Vipond, D. (1998). The researcher as missionary: Problems with rhetoric and reform in the disciplines. *College Composition and Communication, 50* (1), 71–90.

Sennett, R. & Cobb, J. (1972). *The hidden injuries of class.* New York: Random House.

Shor, I. (Ed.). (1987). *Freire for the classroom: A sourcebook for liberatory teaching.* Portsmouth, NH: Boynton/Cook.

Smith, F. (1982). *Writing and the writer.* New York: Holt, Rinehart, & Winston.

Sternglass, M. (1997). *Time to know them: A longitudinal study of writing and learning at the college level.* Mahwah, NJ: Erlbaum.

Stockton, S. (1995). Writing in history: Narrating the subject of time. *Written Communication, 12* (1), 47–73.

Stuckey, E. (1991). *The violence of literacy.* Portsmouth, NH: Boynton/Cook.

Tinberg, H. (2001). Are we good enough? Critical literacy and the working class. *College English, 63* (3), 353–360.

Troyka, L. (1987). Defining basic writing in context. In T. Enos (Ed.), *A sourcebook for basic writing teachers* (pp. 2–15). New York: Random House.

Villanueva, V. (1993). *Bootstraps: From an American academic of color.* Urbana, IL: NCTE.

Vygotsky, L. (1978). *Mind in society: The development of higher psychological processes.* Cambridge, MA: Harvard University Press.

Walvoord, B. (1996). The future of WAC. *College English, 58* (1), 58–79.

Walvoord, B. & McCarthy, L. (1990). *Thinking and writing in college: A naturalistic study of students in four disciplines.* Urbana, IL: NCTE.

Witte, S. P. & Flach, J. (1994). Advanced ability to communicate. *Assessing Writing, 1* (2), 207–246.

Yancey, K. (1997). Teacher portfolios: Lessons in resistance, readiness, and reflection. In K. Yancey & I. Weiser (Eds.), *Situating portfolios: Four perspectives* (pp. 245–262). Logan, UT: Utah State University Press.

Yancey, K. & Huot, B. (Eds.). (1997). *Assessing writing across the curriculum: Diverse approaches and practices.* Greenwich, CT: Ablex.

Yancey, K. & Weiser, I. (Eds.). (1997). *Situating portfolios: Four perspectives.* Logan, UT: Utah State University Press.

Index

academic conventions, xvi, 137; adaptation to, 47, 89–90; contradictory expectations, 7, 26–27; genres, 93–94; student acceptance of, 108–9, 140
academic disciplines, xvi, 58; disciplinary conflicts, 108–9; portfolios used in, 131–32; relevance of requirements, 139–40; writing and literacy across, 5–8. *See also* subcommunities
academic writing, 64; faculty views of, 26–27, 60; student perception of, as "real" writing, 77–78
African American students, 19, 40, 70–71, 101
Alberti, John, 30
American Association of Higher Education (AAHE), 42–43
analytical writing, 76–77
Applebee, A., 91
apprenticeships, 106–8
art history papers, 58–59, 112
Assessing Writing (journal), xiii
assessment, xiii, xvi, 88, 125–29; of portfolios, 127–28; self-assessment, 33, 45, 51, 90, 98; standardized tests, 9–10, 12, 92, 127. *See also* grades
assessment movement, 42–43
Assessment Office web site, 149
assignments. *See* writing assignments
audience, 75, 113–14; approaches to, 65, 66, 139–41
audit of writing, 50–55, 130–32

basic skills, xii, 73–74, 86, 113
basic writers, 29
Bean, J., 141

"Berkeley Guidelines," 62
Bizzell, Patricia, 7
book reviews, 21
Britton, James, 6–7, 23
Brodkey, Linda, 7
Bronfenbrenner, Urie, xiv–xv, 22–23, 47, 85, 88, 115, 129
Brooke, R., 65
Brueggemann, Brenda, 36
Bruner, Jerome, xv, 22, 24–25, 78, 90, 120
business majors, 42

Cannibal Galaxy, The (Ozick), 144
career-oriented programs, 31, 32, 69
case studies, 107
CD–ROM Portfolio Assessment Project, 34, 149–51. *See also* Digital Portfolio Assessment Project
challenge, as necessary to development, 25, 55, 83–84, 134–37
check-sheets, 98, 136
Chiseri-Strater, E., 7
citation style, 103
citizenship, 32, 120, 133–34
class issues, 38–39, 141–42
cognitive development, 48
Cole, Michael, xv, 22, 23, 24, 91, 125, 127, 128–29
Collision Course (Durst), 66–67
commentary and corrections, 12, 15–17, 19, 79, 81, 116–17, 136–37; as context dependent, 95–101
communication majors, 40, 89, 92–93
community. *See* learning community
composition specialists, xi, 61; as advocates, 144–45; missionary role, 28, 91. *See also* faculty

LEE ANN CARROLL is a professor and director of composition at Pepperdine University, where she teaches in the writing and rhetoric emphasis program in English and in the undergraduate teacher-credential program. She is also chair of the advisory board of the California Writing Project, an affiliate of the National Writing Project. She has published in *College Composition and Communication* and in *College English*.

Studies in Writing & Rhetoric

In 1980 the Conference on College Composition and Communication established the Studies in Writing & Rhetoric (SWR) series as a forum for monograph-length arguments or presentations that engage general compositionists. SWR encourages extended essays or research reports addressing any issue in composition and rhetoric from any theoretical or research perspective as long as the general significance to the field is clear. Previous SWR publications serve as models for prospective authors; in addition, contributors may propose alternate formats and agendas that inform or extend the field's current debates.

SWR is particularly interested in projects that connect the specific research site or theoretical framework to contemporary classroom and institutional contexts of direct concern to compositionists across the nation. Such connections may come from several approaches, including cultural, theoretical, field-based, gendered, historical, and interdisciplinary. SWR especially encourages monographs by scholars early in their careers, by established scholars who wish to share an insight or exhortation with the field, and by scholars of color.

The SWR series editor and editorial board members are committed to working closely with prospective authors and offering significant developmental advice for encouraged manuscripts and prospectuses. Editorships rotate every five years. Prospective authors intending to submit a prospectus during the 1997 to 2002 editorial appointment should obtain submission guidelines from Robert Brooke, SWR editor, University of Nebraska-Lincoln, Department of English, P.O. Box 880337, 202 Andrews Hall, Lincoln, NE 68588-0337.

General inquiries may also be addressed to Sponsoring Editor, Studies in Writing & Rhetoric, Southern Illinois University Press, P.O. Box 3697, Carbondale, IL 62902-3697.